YOUR LIFE
Oughta Be A Book

Write the stories of your life.

by

Carol P. Purroy

Carol Petersen Purroy

Published by
A-Z Publications
100 W. Pueblo Street
Reno, NV, 89509

Design and layout by
CPPC Design

Library of Congress Catalog Number: 2001093912

Looking to the past, present and future:

In loving memory of my parents,
Arthur and Zelpha,

with love to my three sons,
Steven, Martin and Alexandre,

my granddaughter, Hannah,

and all the others to whom I am
"Mom" or "Grandma Carol."

ACKNOWLEDGEMENTS:

With enormous gratitude I acknowledge my editors (in alphabetical order) for their invaluable encouragement, suggestions and corrections:

> Bruce L. Allen
> Ronald V. Allen
> Lawrence E. Green
> Mary Madsen Hallock
> Carol McConkie

And to those who so graciously contributed autobiographical excerpts:

> Bruce L. Allen
> Ronald V. Allen
> Ed Alterman
> Freddie Mae Baxter (Knopf Publishing)
> Walter Cronkite (Knopf Publishing)
> Jackson Crooks Clarke
> Sue Denim
> Oliver Green
> Mary Madsen Hallock
> Will James (Scribner & Sons)
> Barbara Jordan (Knopf Publishing)
> Effie Marie Larsen
> Jeann Olson McDuffie
> James Walters
> Leta Inlow Fairfield Wright

And I thank Dover Clip Art Series books for providing most of the book's illustrations. (Dover Publications, Inc., Mineola, NY.)

TABLE OF CONTENTS

— — —

*AE = Autobiographical Excerpt

Directory of Quotes

Carol Petersen Purroy

> *Every time an elder dies
> a library is lost.*
>
> African proverb

PREFACE

The proverb on the opposite page says it all.

All our lives we've been told, "You can't take it with you." But think about it and you'll realize just what a lot you *will* take with you.

You'll take with you everything you've learned, everything you've experienced, everything you've figured out or discovered over the course of your life.

You'll take with you all your skills and talents, your personal history and your family's history. You'll take with you all your knowledge of your era.

You'll take with you your personality, your character, your sense of humor, your values . . . your uniqueness.

Think about all that your ancestors took with them -- in most cases, their entire 'libraries'. But wouldn't you just love to know about your grandparents and great-grandparents and even more distant ancestors -- their dreams; their proudest accomplishments?

Wouldn't you love to know how they endured their hardships and overcame obstacles?

Wouldn't you love to know how and why they made their life-altering decisions?

Wouldn't you love to know their love stories?

Wouldn't you love to know how they felt about and responded to the events and issues of their day?

Wouldn't you love to have a window into what made them laugh, what made them cry . . . what made them 'tick'?

Psychologists tell us that a large part of our sense of Self, our identity, comes from knowing about our heritage. Our ancestors are part of us. We have their DNA. A lot of who we are is because of them. Wouldn't it be wonderful if we could connect with them through their stories, letters, essays, etc., and learn what we have in common with them?

Well, ***they*** may have taken their 'library' with them, but ***you*** don't have to. There's still time for you to create your legacy. It may be the most important thing you'll ever write, maybe even more important than your will, which is, after all, only about money and material things. Think about this:

> *Most of the important things in life are not things.*

It's possible that the most important thing you can leave behind is your 'library' -- the story of YOU.

INTRODUCTION

My parents died young, before I had a chance to get their stories. And it left a big hole in my life. I **want** to know about my mom and dad, but they're gone and there's no one I can ask. There's an avalanche of things I don't know. I don't know how they met and fell in love. I don't know what they enjoyed doing, other than dancing -- I'm told that they were terrific dancers. I know very little about their childhoods; their school years. I don't know about their dreams, their plans for the future. There's so much I don't know -- can never know.

I wish I could step back in time and learn more about my parents and grandparents -- and *their* parents and grandparents. There are photographs of the 2 generations before me, for which I am very grateful. But I'd love to know the stories that go with those photos. And I'd love to know more about the earlier generations, those who were not photographed, those who are just names and dates on a genealogy chart. It's nice to know that much, but I want their **stories,** too! I want to know who my ancestors were, what made them laugh, what made them cry . . . what made them tick.

I wonder why my two sets of grandparents left their homelands, their family and friends, and why they settled in California's Central Valley. I wonder what it was like for them when they arrived and settled in. Was it what they expected? How did they cope with being young and on their own in a strange land? How did they develop a support system there? What did they do to survive, both physically and emotionally?

I'd love to have just a scrap of paper written by (or about) them or some earlier ancestors that would give me a glimpse into their lives.

This project -- first the class and now the book and the DVD/Video class -- grew out of that. I started teaching the class back in 1991 because I don't want that to happen to others. I want all of you to pass on as much of yourselves as you can so your children and grandchildren will know you.

Here's a sobering thought: If you have offspring, you will someday be someone's distant ancestor. They will be thrilled to know about you if you write your stories, and conversely, will feel the lack if you don't.

If you don't have offspring, there are others who will be interested in knowing about you and your era.

Whether you are writing your stories for family and friends or for a much broader audience, this book is for you.

ABOUT THIS BOOK

◆ Throughout this book are autobiographical excerpts for your enjoyment, to jog your memory, and to make the point that in writing your life stories, anything goes. Any subject you can think of is grist for the literary mill.

Included are stories and poems by several people. They may or may not be related to the subject in the previous or subsequent sections. Some are there merely for your reading enjoyment.

◆ I apologize for overwhelming you with my own stories. Before you finish this book you will know a lot about me, more than you ever wanted to, I'm sure. I hope you can take the examples and use them for your own purposes.

◆ Writing Activities are scattered throughout the book. They are merely suggestions. I find that some people like to have "assignments" so I've included them to get you started if you're one of those people.
If you're not, more power to you. Go for it.

◆ The Appendix contains a couple of word lists: *'90 ways to say "said"'*, and 3 pages of *'emotion-words'*. Check them out. It contains additional 'Writing Activities', too.

◆ In this book, I use *autobiography, life story* & *memoir* interchangeably. Technically, an *autobiography* is an overview of one's life, starting with, "I was born . . ."; a *memoir* is a piece of one's life, based on a theme or particular slant, or covering a specific period or adventure; and a *life story* is just what the name implies, a story -- any story of any length and depth -- from one's life.

In this book, however, the terms are synonymous.

Planning to write is not writing.
Outlining a book is not writing.
Researching is not writing.
Talking to people about what you're doing,
none of that is writing.
Writing is writing.

E.L. Doctorow

YOUR LIFE OUGHTA BE A BOOK

Your life oughta be a book. And, boy, have you got stories to tell! You don't have to have been an astronaut, a bank robber, a movie star or a 'madam' to have stories worth writing about. *Your* life is exotic!

It's possible that you don't think of your life as anything out of the ordinary. And maybe, for your time and place, it hasn't been all that unusual. But you're writing for future generations about what it was like to be a child, a teenager, a young adult, and even a mature adult in a time they can't even imagine. So far as they're concerned, it's like a visit to another planet.

You'll be telling them what your school, profession, hometown and family were like in *the olden days*. You'll be telling about kitchen appliances and work implements and toys that will amaze and amuse them. You'll be writing about pastimes and adventures of a bygone time. You'll be cluing them in on the fads and fancies of your era. That's exotic!

You'll be placing historic events in a very personal light and, by doing so, you'll allow your readers to learn things that won't be found in any history book.

When history books tell us about a war, for example, we learn the goals of both sides, the names of the top generals, the dates and locations of the major battles, and which side won. (Yawn.)

However, by placing individuals and families in those events and bringing to light their personalities, goals, thoughts, emotions, experiences -- their triumphs and tragedies -- we not only learn a lot about that war, we also find ourselves *caring* about its events and their outcome, as well as the characters themselves.

If you're like me, when you get to 'know' the people involved, you care about them. You live vicariously through them: you weep when they're sad; you smile when they're happy; you laugh out loud at their foibles. Their goals are your goals, their adventures are yours, too, at least, until you read **The End** and close the book or leave the theater.

So it is when you place yourself, your family and friends (and enemies) in a certain timeframe. You are teaching your readers about your era, its events and the people who lived through them in a way that really grabs them. You'll get them involved in very personal historical accounts -- yours.

What were your experiences of *your* war eras? WWII? The Korean War? The Vietnam War? The Persian Gulf War? Whether you were in the trenches, dodging bullets, or at home serving doughnuts at the USO -- or protesting your country's involvement -- it affected your life and influenced you.

More recently, where were you and what were you doing on "9/11", when the World Trade Center and the Pentagon were attacked by terrorists? What were your thoughts and emotions as you watched it happen or learned about it? What affect has it had on your life?

And what about the other major social- and culture-changing periods of your lifetime, e.g: the Great Depression, the Labor Movement, the Holocaust, the Cold War/ McCarthy Era, the 'Fabulous Fifties', the Civil Rights Movement, the Counterculture/Flowerchild Era, the Sexual Revolution, Women's Liberation, the Space Race, the AIDS epidemic, the Drug Culture, the Environmental Movement? And now, the Age of Terrorism? What was (is) your participation? How have you and your life changed because of them?

And what about the inventions and innovations of your lifetime? Such things as wonder drugs, automatic washers and dryers, television, contraceptive pills, jumbo jets, microsurgery, digital cameras, central heating & air conditioning, computers and the internet, luggage-on-wheels, cell phones, and so on?

What impact has any of them had on your life? How? Why?

Boy, have you got stories to tell!

HISTORY'S MYSTERIES

Remember that old philosophical question: *If a tree falls in the forest and there's no one there to hear it, does it make a sound?*

Well, how about this one: *If you lived on this planet but no one here knows anything about you, who gives a good 'Gee Whiz'?*

Oh, some people care . . . . **now**. But a generation or two into the future, who will know . . . . or care? Fifty or a hundred years from now, you'll just be one of history's mysteries, having faded into anonymity and obscurity . . . .. unless you write your stories.

Marco Polo is a name familiar to most of us. But who was he? A 13th century teenager from Venice, Italy, who tagged along with a group of tradesmen on a trip to China. So, why do we know about him but not the others who went before, with or after him? Because he wrote his story, that's why!

He told of his incredible adventures and discoveries, informing current (13th century) and future generations about himself and his era. The others did not.

This adolescent who was just along for the ride stole their thunder. He's the one we know about. Perhaps the adults he accompanied had great influence at that time, but because they didn't write their stories they are just a footnote in history -- an anonymous, obscure footnote.

Don't be like them. And don't be like that tree, falling (perhaps) silently in the forest. *Make some noise! Exclaim yourself! Pronounce yourself! Celebrate your life!*

Your readers, whoever they may be, will want to know you: your character, your values, your quirks, your passions, your philosophy, your sense of humor, your accomplishments, your philanthropies, your adventures and misadventures, your adversities, your adversaries, your struggles, your complexities, what makes you tick, what interests you, what excites you, who you fell in love with, how you chose your career(s), why you moved from one part of the world to another, what you have learned about life, *et cetera*.

Like Marco Polo, leave a record of your life and times for current and future generations.

(Of course, you may want parts of your history to remain a mystery. That's okay. You're entitled.)

WONDER IF YOU'RE UP TO IT?

You may look upon the task of writing your life stories with dread or even horror. Perhaps you don't know where to begin or how to go about it. You will, no doubt, want to write stories or a book that people will enjoy reading, a page-turner they won't be able to put down.

You will want to write it in such a way that people will enjoy reading it, not just because they know you and love you, but because it's a good read on its own merits. But you may wonder if you're up to it.

Chances are, you're not a writer, or haven't been up 'til now. Maybe you're not the world's best speller, and your grammar ain't exactly the Queen's English. Your vocabulary may not be the equal of a Fullbright Scholar's.

No matter. Help is at hand. The purpose of this book is to make the job easier for you. But equally important, it is to help you create a finished product that's captivating. In the pages that follow you'll find a lot of tips on how to accomplish that.

WHO IN THEIR RIGHT MIND WRITES AN AUTOBIOGRAPHY?

Fortunately, an autobiography is not one of those documents that customarily begins, "Being of sound mind, I . . . " Writing autobiographically has no such requirement, so go for it, regardless of your state of mind.

More and more people are now thinking about writing their life stories, and actually doing it. Whether they're in their right mind matters not a whit. But since they are contemplating it and doing it, many are finding that they could use a little help and a little encouragement.

This book's appeal is probably mostly to people in their later years, simply because that group now has time to sit down, cogitate, reflect and write.

Also, members of this group have reached the point in life at which they can look back and reflect, placing things in perspective and trying to make some sense out of it. I call it the "'What's it all about, Alfie?' syndrome."

They are discovering that they want to pass on to others what they have spent a lifetime learning.

They are finding that they want to leave something meaningful behind. And, let's face it, most people will never have a monument erected or an airport named in their honor, so autobiography is the thing.

They may be seeking a new purpose in life, or simply a purposeful way to fill their time, their formal careers having come to an end. And writing the stories of their lives fills the bill.

They are often encouraged (i.e., nagged) by their kids and grandkids to tell their stories. And they really do want to know about their ancestors, so don't be recalcitrant. Just do it, for them.

However, people of all ages, like our 13th century teenager, Marco Polo, can and should be recording their life experiences, as well as their thoughts and emotions about the events of their lives. (The day-by-day events of our lives are history in the making, a fact we tend to forget.) This may be done in the form of letters to a good friend (if you email them, make a copy for yourself and file them), or a journal. It can be newspaper clippings or favorite books, with notes scribbled in the margins. These will prove invaluable later on when you want to sit down and write your own history.

In this little book is a list of topics to help spark ideas, some of which you may wish to include in your writings. It also includes a variety of approaches to writing your own stories. There are helpful hints on making it less a dry-as-dust history lesson and more a juicy tale of flesh-and-blood people.

This book is for all autobiographers: those who simply want to write little bits-and-pieces as well as those who will pen full-fledged books, novels or plays, and everyone in between. Do not be intimidated, thinking you must write volumes. To qualify as an autobiographer you need only write something -- *anything* -- about your own life or your family's.

Your Life Oughta Be A Book is for autobiographers at all levels. I invite you to take from it what you need, whatever fits. If parts of it do not apply to you or your project, simply discard them. In your stories you want your uniqueness to come through, so there are no hard and fast rules.

Do not allow yourself to become stressed by writing your life story. Let yourself have fun in the reminiscing and the telling of it.

What is needed for this task is for you to get into your ***write mind*** and don't give your ***right mind*** a second thought.

WHAT TO WRITE ABOUT

Writers sometimes get stuck or have a hard time getting started writing in the first place. The task of writing about one's life can seem overwhelming.

Starting on the next page is an extensive yet partial list of suggested story topics. Not all will apply to everyone, of course. It is offered only to introduce possible subjects for inclusion in your memoirs. There is no suggestion that you try to incorporate all, or even most, of them in your autobiography.

Throughout the book are examples of a few of these topics, compiled from both published and unpublished autobiographies. I recommend reading them just to get an inkling of what is possible. They are entertaining and informative -- a good read. And they may give you ideas for your own stories.

While the list is quite long it's only a fraction of the topics you could include in your life story. It's just to get you started thinking. You may choose to write an entire story or anecdote on a single topic, or merely to mention it in passing.

TOPICS

- Recollections/legends about relatives: parents, siblings, grandparents, other ancestors, aunts, uncles, cousins, etc.
- Your child(ren) and grandchild(ren): their birth, infancy and childhood. How each one is special.
- Adoptees: Your search for and/or discovery of your birth parent(s), or why you chose not to search for them.
- Your relationship with your parent(s), as a child -- or as an adult.
- Your most heartwarming, terrifying or tragic memory.
- What you hoped your parents would never find out about, and what happened if they did.
- Your family's superstitions and/or customs.
- How illness was treated in your family.
- Holidays: Your family's, neighborhood's or culture's customs and traditions.
- How a family tradition started.
- Where you were and what you were doing when you felt most *alive*.
- Adventures, travels.
- Your enemy(ies).
- Your hero(es).
- Risks you took, or wish you had taken.
- Historical events. Where you were, what you were doing, how it impacted your life when:
    - A war began or ended
    - An important person died
    - Natural disaster (hurricane, earthquake, flood, fire,

tornado, ice storm) struck.
- Memories of a socio-political movement.
- A turning point.
- Your romances. The love of your life:
    - How you met
    - What attracted you
    - How you managed to get together
- Your heartbreaks.
- The most romantic moment of your life.
- Rites of passage. Coming-of-age rites.
- Sex education. Who taught you about sex? How?
- First date. First kiss. First sexual experience.
- Your greatest disappointment.
- Challenges, obstacles you overcame (or didn't).
- The most bizarre or unusual experience of your life.
- The most courageous thing you've ever done.
- The thing you're most proud of.
- Things you wish you could change.
- "If I knew then what I know now . . ."
- Your mistakes; what you learned from them.
- Good friends. Important people in your life.
- Jobs: the first, the worst, the best, the weirdest, the most fulfilling, the most fun, etc.
- How/why you chose your career(s).
- Your spiritual journey:
    - Your spiritual philosophy
    - How you got to where you are now, spiritually
    - The impact it has had on your life

- An epiphany
- (Best/Worse) Advice you were given.
- Your politics:
  - Your political philosophy and/or affiliation.
  - Your political/social activism.
  - How you got to where you are now, politically.
- Your concerns, pursuits, missions, purpose.
- Disobedience, civil or uncivil.
- Pets.
- "As my (e.g., parent) used to say . . . "
- How your parents (or surrogates) raised you: what was important to them. How you raised your children differently -- or the same.
- How you were taught values.
- How you were named.
- How you got your nickname.
- A humiliation or embarrassment.
- Your special talents, skills, attributes.
- Clubs, organizations you've belonged to.
- The ironies of your life.
- The smartest or dumbest thing you've ever done.
- Health and accidents. Experiences with doctors and hospitals.
- Wealth and/or poverty in your life.
- Food, special meals, recipes.
- Fragrances, aromas that elicit memories.
- Music, songs, concerts, instruments; Dancing.
- Radio & TV shows.

- Movies and movie stars.
- Fads.
- Toys.
- Cars.
- Clothes, shoes, hats.
- Furniture.
- Jewelry.
- Inventions or innovations.
- Sports.
- What it was like being a child in your era; who you were as a child:
    - What you enjoyed doing.
    - How you spent summer days.
    - School days.
    - Dreams, fantasies.
    - Friends.
    - Games you played, songs you sang.
    - Artifacts of the period.
- What it was like being a teenager in your era. (See above list.)
- Who you were as a young adult:
    - Leaving home.
    - College/University days.
    - Military duty.
    - Relationships (friends, love affairs, etc.).
    - Jobs.
    - Dreams, goals, fantasies, plans for the future.
- An unforgettable character. Someone who influenced

you.

- Being maligned, treated or judged unfairly.
- Being betrayed (or betraying someone else).
- Abuses/tortures you endured.
- The nicest/worst thing anyone's ever done for/to you.
- The best/worst day of your life.
- The best gift anyone ever gave you.
- Your hobbies; collections.
- Your brush with celebrity.
- A brush with death; a near-death experience.
- Miracles, angels, divine intervention.
- Kismet - Destiny - Fate; serendipity, synchronicity.
- A supernatural or paranormal experience:
  - Visits/Messages from beyond the grave.
  - Ghosts.
  - "Invisible friends."
  - An out-of-body experience.
  - Extraterrestrial sightings, experiences.
- Loss, grief, bereavement, healing.
- Something you cannot forgive of another.
- Something you'd like to be forgiven for.
- Your life's mission or purpose.
- How life turned out different than you expected.
- Regrets:
  - What you did that you wish you hadn't.
  - What you didn't do that you wish you had.
- The biggest lie you ever told -- and the consequences.
- Your health (medical) history -- including whatever you

know about your ancestors' health history. (This could be part of a section on genealogy. While it is probably not the most exciting to your general audience, it is vital to your descendants.)

As you can see, the possibilities are infinite. I'm sure you can add to this list.

In the next section are further   suggestions on where to get ideas for subjects to write about. Write about whatever comes to mind. The important thing is to get going and just do it.

THE IMWALLE HOUSE

Mary Madsen Hallock, Santa Rosa, CA

. . . Spring Street was not as fancy as McDonald Avenue, one block over, but it was a very nice neighborhood. Both streets were paved all the way from Fourth Street to one block shy of the rural cemetery. That last block, where the Presbyterian Church is now, was a big vacant lot shaded with elm trees. Every summer a huge tent was pitched under the trees, and the "Holy Rollers" held a camp meeting there. From our house we could hear them singing hymns and clapping in time to the music. That lot was at the edge of town. Beyond it were prune orchards and the countryside.

The cross streets, 13th, 14th, 15th and 16th, were not paved. A horse and wagon went up and down them delivering ice once or twice a week. Mother had a red card she put in the window if we needed ice. The position of the card indicated how many pounds she wanted, and the ice man would use his tongs to carry in the right-sized chunk and put it into our icebox on the screened back porch.

Mr. Imwalle plied a route through the neighborhood, too, with a wagon filled with the vegetables he raised on his farm out west of town. He'd drive by slowly, shouting, "Wedge-tobbles," and the ladies would come out and buy from him.

Each block had an alley through its center, parallel to

McDonald and Spring, with all the barns and back yards opening onto the alleys. Every morning, after the husbands went off to work, the housewives on Spring and McDonald would trot up and down the alleys, having coffee at each other's house.

One day, according to my father, Mr. Imwalle hitched his horse and vegetable wagon to the rail in front of the Exchange Bank and went inside to ask Mr. LeBaron about a large house on McDonald Avenue that was for sale.

"I'm afraid it's more than you can afford," Mr. LeBaron said kindly. "It's twelve hundred dollars."

Mr. Imwalle didn't answer. He just turned on his heel and left. But he returned immediately with two heavy buckets which he placed on Mr. LeBaron's desk.

"If dot's not enough, I got two more oudt in der vagon," he said. The buckets were filled with gold coins.

When the Imwalles moved into their new house, the ladies of McDonald Avenue were all a-twitter about whether or not to call on the wife of their "wedge-tobble" man. They did, of course, and the house is still known as The Imwalle House -- at least to us oldtimers.

Remember -- You Asked For It!, self-published. 2000

WHERE TO GET IDEAS

At any point in writing your life stories, you may experience a bit of a slowdown. Following are some sure-fire resources to spur you on:

• **Family Albums**. You'll see photographs of yourself, your family and friends; of holidays, celebrations, rites of passage, ceremonies, vacations, etc., and memories will come in a deluge. Every photo has a story.

• **Scrapbooks**. Every item in a scrapbook was placed there to remind you at some future time about the good times you had: special events, vacations, holidays, *et cetera*. So every page is filled with stories for you to write.

• **Music.** As you listen to music from your past, certain pieces will remind you of another time -- a romantic time, a poignant time, a triumphant time, a time of terror, a time of sadness. Music has the power to transport us through time and space better than almost anything else.

• **A Reunion**. As you see and talk with old friends,

colleagues and relatives at a reunion, you'll be inundated with memories, some of which you may want to write about. Chances are, you'll learn new information or added tidbits that may be worthy of inclusion in your memoirs.

• **Fragrance, Aroma, Scent.** Fragrance is *the* most powerful memory jogger of all. Aromas of food and flowers -- scents reminiscent of another time and place -- bring back memories, sensations and emotions.

• **Movies & TV Shows**. Oftentimes something in a movie or TV show, especially period pieces, reminds us of something in our own history: a situation, a relationship, an artifact, toy, old car or airplane, a piece of furniture or clothing, or even a painting on the wall in the film.

• **Household items: Furniture, books, china, silver, *objets d'art,* toys, jewelry.** Look around your house at the furniture and knickknacks. Poke around in the attic, basement, cedar chest, china cabinet, bookcase, jewelry box. You're bound to find several items with stories.

• **Cookbooks, Recipe Boxes.** You'll recall special meals, special occasions and special people as you go through your cookbooks and recipe files. Many of our pleasantest (and some of our awfulest) memories are associated with food and cooking.

• **Other People's Life Stories.** As you read other people's biographies and autobiographies or hear others' life stories, you'll think of incidents, people or places that you'll want to write about. They're great memory-joggers.

You never know from whence inspiration will come, so, in addition to checking through the "What To Write About" list and the "Where To Get Ideas" resources from time to time, I urge you to keep your antennae receptive and allow yourself to reminisce wherever you go.

My sister Pat and I recently attended a cousin's funeral and encryptment in a marble mausoleum. I poked Pat with my elbow and whispered, "Does this place remind you of anything?" She nodded and whispered back. Sure enough, her association was the same as mine, based on a very peculiar ritual in our childhood. It got me thinking and I realized it was an anecdote I could write up. ('A Bizarre Ritual', on page 53.)

When I have trouble writing, I step outside my studio into the garden and pull weeds until my mind clears -- I find weeding to be the best therapy there is for writer's block.

Irving Stone

Writing Activity:

Look through a family photo album or scrapbook for a story idea.

◆ Pretend you're showing the album to someone, a grandchild, for instance. As you come to a photo or memento that brings back memories, you'll want to tell him or her about it: what was going on at that time; what you remember about the day that photo was taken or what other associations you have regarding it.

◆ That's your story! Write it.

◆ Have fun!

Travel tales

AMERICANS DON'T RIDE BIKES

Ed Alterman, Palm Springs, CA

Bicycles were available at our hotel in Tai Shan, China, and we wanted to go for a ride. Bikes were the standard form of transportation in China and we wanted to experience the area as the locals did. Everybody rides bikes. In 1981 in China, even in big cities, the ratio of bikes to cars was at least 1000 to 1.

We'd been assigned two tour guides, "old Mr. Lee" and "young Mr. Lee," who were our constant companions. They were with us ostensibly for our protection and assistance and their approval was necessary for everything we did.

We were the first non-Chinese to visit that part of China in more than thirty years, after Chairman Mao's long reign, and were mobbed by locals everywhere we went. They were not unfriendly, just extremely curious about the strange creatures from afar. We were to learn that they had some strange notions about us.

As I said, we wanted to go biking in the countryside in and around Tai Shan, but the Misters Lee refused to give us their permission.

"Why?"

"Americans can't ride bikes," one answered.

"What? Why would you think that?"

"Americans all drive cars. Americans can't ride bikes."

"Of course we ride bikes," we insisted. "And we want

to! Today."

The Misters Lee were certain bike-riding Americans would cause accidents on the city streets and country roads. At our insistence we were allowed to prove our competence. We were to ride around the small lake behind our hotel -- on an off-road walking trail -- <u>twice</u> without incident. Only then would we be allowed out on the streets and roads. We had no choice but to comply. They watched closely as we peddled twice around the lake. Though disinclined, they gave their approval.

As it turned out, they were right. We *were* the cause of accidents. The good people of Tai Shan, riding their bicycles to and from work, to and from market, to and from school, to and from business and medical appointments, were so amazed to see Americans on bikes that they forgot to look where they were going. They ran into each other left and right. There was chaos at every corner!

We decided that the real reason they didn't want us riding bikes was that we'd be more difficult to control if we were to travel in any way other than *en masse* in the China Tourism Office's minibus.

And it's true, once we had our own wheels, the ten of us scattered in nearly as many directions. And off sightseeing individually, away from the watchful eyes of the ever-present Misters Lee, we enjoyed ourselves more than any other time on the trip, like kids let out of school.

*Published in **55-plus!**, San Francisco, CA. 1997*

THE TIMELINE OF YOUR LIFE

Another approach to writing your life stories and thinking of things to write about is The Timeline of Your Life. Here's what you do:

Get a piece of paper and draw a line across it. Divide the line into segments representing different periods of your life. These segments can be in terms of age, places you lived, schools/grade levels, significant events, sociological periods, jobs/careers, relationships, or whatever designations work for you.

An Age Timeline might look like this:

The first segment is the period between birth and age 6. The second is between 6 and 12; the third, 12 to 16; the fourth, 16 to 20, and so on, or however you want to do it.

Choose a segment of your timeline and think about an event or situation, a person, place or thing (or all of the above) during that time period. Use the Balloon Method (in the next section) to remember everything you can about it, then write your story.

A School Timeline might look something like this:

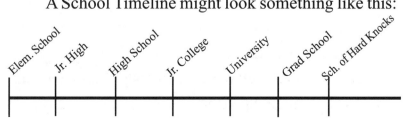

Pick one and let your mind wander backwards to the time period you've selected. There are dozens of stories that will come to mind in any one of them. Your story doesn't have to have anything to do with school. Your timeline could simply serve to remind you of something that happened during that time period.

A Sociological Era Timeline could look something like this:

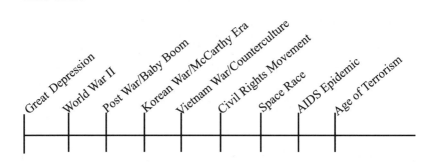

The eras you choose may be different from mine. Go with yours. It's your story, remember? Each of the time periods on your timeline will bring to mind an abundance of memories and stories.

The Timeline of Your Life is a powerful method of recollecting memories from a particular period.

This is a good exercise for a memoir-writing class or writers' group, e.g: in the third timeline above, everyone in the group could write about the Vietnam War/Counterculture era. You'll be amazed at the wide range of experiences that are written up in any group.

One member may write about his/her child (or oneself) who got caught up in the 'Tune In, Turn On, Drop out' phenomenon of the '60s and '70s; another might tell about being a policeman who arrested war protesters; another might write about being a war protester; and another about being a college or university student at that time; one might tell about his/her military experience in Vietnam -- or about a loved one who fought and/or died in that war, and so on. Everyone who lived through that era has a story -- or many -- to tell about it. Expect a wide range of emotions to surface, too.

Any timeline you use will reap rich rewards. It's a great way to elicit memories. And you'll find that once you start remembering it's easy to get those memories down on paper or disk.

Writing Activity:

Write about an event in your life, between the ages of 6 and 12.

◆ This is a time rich with memories . . . and stories. It covers our entire elementary school experience so there are the schoolyard bullies, the sweet kids, the 'best friend', teachers, music lessons, church/temple, games, toys, hobbies, activities, radio/TV shows, movies, your parents and siblings, plus whatever was going on in the world at that time. (For me, World War II was in the background so a lot of my kid stories have that association.)

◆ Let your mind drift until you remember something that happened during that time.

◆ Write about it.

◆ Have fun!

Fads; Fashions

GRANDMA SHOES
author unknown

When I was very little, all the grandmas that I knew
all walked around this world in ugly grandma shoes.
You know the ones I speak of, those black clunky-heeled kind.
They looked so very awful that it weighed upon my mind,
for I knew, when I grew old I'd have to wear those shoes.
I'd think of that from time to time,
it seemed like such bad news.
I never was a rebel; I wore saddle shoes to school,
and next came ballerinas, then the sandals, pretty cool,
and then came spikes with pointed toes,
then platforms, very tall.
As each new fashion came along I wore them, one and all.
But always, in the distance, looming in my future, there
was that awful pair of ugly shoes,
the kind that grandmas wear.
I eventually got married, and then became a mom,
our kids grew up and left, and when their children came along,
I knew I was a grandma and the time was drawing near
when those clunky, black, old lace-up shoes
were what I'd have to wear.
How would I do my gardening or take my morning hike?
I couldn't even start to think how I would ride my bike!
But fashions kept evolving and one day I realized
that the shape of things-to-come
had changed before my very eyes.
And now, when I go shopping what I see fills me with glee
for in my jeans and Reeboks, I'm comfy as can be.
I look at all the teenage girls, and there upon their feet
are clunky, black, old grandma shoes
and they think they're really neat!

FOOD AS A 'STORY STARTER'

It's a fact that many of us cook, and all of us eat. Food is a constant in all our lives and we all have a favorite food or recipe. All of us have memories associated with food, from snatching a pre-dinner taste in Grandma's kitchen to perhaps an elegant dinner in a posh restaurant or on an ocean liner. Maybe you had an memorable dinner in a far-off land, or you learned to love a particular dish you first tasted on your travels.

Food is a terrific memory-jogger. A dish or recipe may be the topic of your story. Or it could just be the trigger that reminds you of an event or adventure and the food will be mentioned as part of the story.

The following anecdote is a perfect example, written by Lawrence ("Lucky Larry") Green of Reno, NV:

The Best Meal I Ever Had

If you have ever reflected on the topic above you may have had some trouble identifying your choice. I did not. I know the answer.

In my 20-plus years in the Air Force, I dined in many places: Paris, London, New York, New Orleans, San Francisco, Honolulu, Tokyo, Singapore, Saigon and Sydney, to drop a few. The "Best Meal I Ever Had" did not occur at any of those. Rather, it was a place you may never had heard of: Thule AFB, Greenland, 600 miles north of the Arctic Circle, the farthest north in the world.

As a young fighter pilot, I was part of our 'first line of defense' against a Russian attack coming over The Pole in 1953, at the height of The Cold War. Temperatures ranged from 25° above to 55° below.

The Air Force may put you in harm's way but they do want you to survive. I had been to desert survival school, jungle survival school, mountain survival school, and now I was going to ice cap survival school.

After a half-day 'training', 10 of us were taken out to the Arctic ice cap and spaced a good distance apart, with only the equipment we flew in with: a backpack parachute and a 15" X 15" seatpack. In it was everything needed to survive a few days, including an ice saw. Each of us was to construct an igloo, then sit tight. They would pick us up in 72 hours.

As it happened, a helluva storm blew in and they couldn't come get us. They didn't show up. And they didn't show up. And they didn't show up. Finally, by the time they got there, I had consumed all my provisions. And I was getting hungry.

I was taken by snowcat to a quonset hut -- a warm, cozy quonset hut. Talk about ambience! The other 9 had been rescued, too, so I was in the company of good friends. We were treated to breakfast. Each of us got 2 stale dough-nuts and 2 ultra-cold Coors beers.

It was definitely the best meal I ever had!

And here's a tidbit from my (autobiographical) cook-book. It accompanies a recipe I got from this friend many years ago:

Agnes Foo, hails from Shanghai, China. She's the

mother of three boys, as am I. We were sort of 2nd-mother to each other's kids. As they were growing up, her middle son, Patrick, did NOT like Chinese food, while my youngest, Alex, absolutely LOVED it.

Whenever Agnes was cooking Chinese food I'd get a phone call from her, saying, "I'm cooking 'Chinese' tonight. Do you want to trade kids?"

So Alex would go across the street to dine on exotic delicacies while Patrick would come to our house for Macaroni & Cheese or Tuna-Noodle Casserole, or whatever we were having, and everyone was happy.

I mentioned my cookbook earlier. This is a book of recipes compiled over the years. I put it together for my sons and granddaughter, but others wanted copies, too. I've made it available on my website as an example of an autobiographical cookbook, to encourage others to create one for their families and friends. I included a very brief 'memoir' with many of the recipes. Sometimes it's just my recollection of the person who gave me the recipe, other times it's about a time that dish was served, and still others, it's about a tradition featuring that dish.

Following is the 'memoir' accompanying the recipe for Orange Rolls:

These delicious rolls were a staple at our holiday dinners. I suspect the recipe goes back many, many generations, maybe all the way back to my maternal ancestors in England. In our family, no holiday dinner was complete without them.

Back when the recipe and the tradition began, oranges were a rare and expensive delicacy for anyone not living in a warm, southern climate.

My mother told of her childhood Christmasses in Missouri. Each child in the family would get just one present. And each one's Christmas stocking would contain a few pieces of hard candy, some nuts and an orange, this last, a huge treat to be savored.

And then, at Christmas dinner, these orange rolls would be the *piece d'resistance.*

In doing 'research' for my cookbook (going through my recipe box and cookbooks which were jammed with newspaper clippings and bits of paper on which recipes were scribbled), I was inundated with memories: people I hadn't thought about in a long time but who have meant so much to me; experiences and even whole eras I'd all but forgotten; dinners, parties and holiday gatherings.

I encourage each of you to dig through your recipes and unearth your own memories -- and write them down for your offspring, and theirs.

Soon to be published is a children's book based on an event in my childhood in which a cookie recipe plays an important part. It will be available on my website, too.

Writing Activity:

Write a story about food or in which food plays a part.

◆ Search your memory banks to find a story about one of the following (or use an idea of your own):
  - The best meal I ever had.
  - The worst meal I ever had.
  - My most romantic meal.
  - My mom's best dish.
  - My dad, the cook.
  - The most exotic (or memorable) meal on my trip to _____.
  - A camping trip: campfire cooking, etc.
  - Growing or picking/gathering your own food.
  - Being hungry.
  - A traditional holiday dish.
  - Grandma's kitchen.
  - Preserving homegrown food: canning, making jams, jellies, pickles, etc.
  - The 1st packaged foods, or cooking from scratch.
  - The most elegant place I've ever dined.
  - Potluck suppers, family gatherings, etc.

You get the idea. You'll have so many options for stories that it will be difficult to pick just one. You may end up with a cookbook of your own (or your writing group's), or an anthology of stories and essays about food.

◆ Have fun!

THE BALLOON METHOD

Once you have decided upon a topic, where do you go from there? The Balloon Method is an excellent way of recollecting everything there is to remember about a person, place or thing, or an event.

Take a piece of paper and write your topic in the center. Draw a circle (balloon) around it.

Then sit quietly for a few moments with your eyes closed, taking deep breaths and exhaling slowly, feeling your body become more relaxed with each breath.

Start thinking about the topic you've selected. The memories will come flooding in.

Open your eyes and grab a pen. As fast as a thought comes to you, jot it down, somewhere on the paper, don't worry about where. Don't censor yourself, even if it seems silly or way off base, or you'll stop the flow.

As you're writing one thing, three others will pop into your head, so just keep writing as fast as you can. Use abbreviations, shorthand or one-word memory-joggers.

When you've exhausted all your memories of that topic, draw a balloon around each one. Look over the balloons and notice which ones are related. You can cluster them in your mind, draw strings attaching them, or color in the balloons with crayons or hi-liter pens, a different color for each cluster. (Some will overlap.) You'll find that you have an abundance of memories and details to draw from. You don't have to use all, or any, of the things you wrote down, but you've got them if you want them.

To illustrate the Balloon Method, I have done the exercise using My Childhood Bedroom (shared with my sister) as my topic. (For this book, I didn't abbreviate or use shorthand as much as I normally would.)

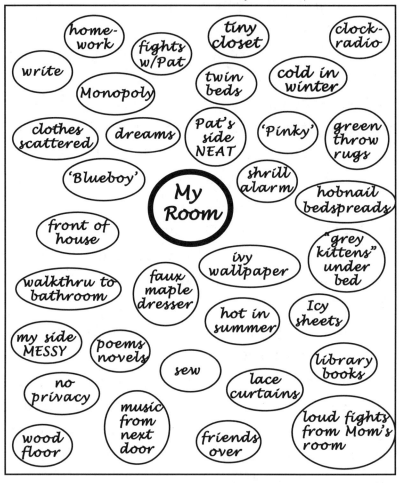

After completing this exercise I have plenty to think about. Now I can select from these many aspects of my room to flesh out stories of my childhood/teenage years.

I used some of these recollections in my children's book (mentioned earlier).

The 'balloon' items were very useful in creating a vivid impression of that room. I hope my readers will get to experience it along with me.

<u>*Recollections of parents*</u>

IT'S TIME WE DANCED

Bruce L. Allen, San Francisco & Petaluma, CA

... My father's background was Baptist, but he did not tolerate what he considered the narrowness of many of the church's positions. Even so, his early religious training stopped him from learning to dance.

On the other side was my mother who was a bit of an Irish colleen when it came to dancing. She had been trained as a young girl to do Irish stepdancing and loved it. No matter how much she prodded, he would not let her teach him how to dance, nor would he even step one foot inside a dance hall. He thought the matter was closed.

There was a woman, however, a close friend of my mother's, named Ethel, who was a war widow at the age of 28. Ethel went to all the local dances. She would be fueling my mother's dreams over a cup of morning tea as she related her dancing nights.

The dancing/anti-dancing scrimmage was on, my father saying *No*, and my mother trying to convince him to say *Yes*.

In a good strategic move my mother announced that if he would not go she would go with her friend, Ethel. He could drive them to the dance and pick them up later to take them home.

Now, my mother was a fine-looking woman and a good dancer. Within the first hour she was dancing every dance. Ethel came to my mother and whispered, "Did you know that Bob is standing 'way over there in the back corner? He looks so sad and alone."

The three-piece orchestra began to play a slow dance, Irving Berlin's *Always.* My mother started across the dance floor heading for the corner where my father was. Several young guys approached her, asking her to dance. She declined, still walking toward my father.

She stood before him and smiled, made just a little bit of an Irish curtsy, and said, "Come, Bob. It's time we danced."

My father became a dancing man that night . . . and for the rest of his life. Ballroom, Latin, Exhibition, Square Dancing, my parents did it all!

One of my most poignant memories was my parents dancing to *Always* at their 50th wedding anniversary party.

Button End Stories, Button End Publ. Co. San Francisco, CA. 2002

FRINGE BENEFITS

My greatest reward as the teacher of memoir-writing classes is to watch my students' growth in competence and confidence. Many of them come nervously to the first class, lacking conviction that their life's experiences are worthy of recording and anxious about their ability to write them.

Through the process of writing their stories and sharing them with their classmates, they come to recognize and acknowledge that they are indeed special, unique individuals and that others really are interested in what they have to say. They become convinced that they can tell their own and their family's stories better than anyone else, and gain the self-assurance to do it.

In the process, they learn that writing is no big deal -- nothing to get all uptight about. They learn that writing and sharing their stories is a lot of fun.

As their classmates validate their life-experiences, an unexpected fringe-benefit becomes apparent. Their self-esteem and sense of self-worth begin to blossom. Then, as they share their stories with their families, whose responses are also positive, their self-regard and self-respect are further enhanced. Their children and grandchildren, their friends and neighbors are impressed with the wonderful, sometimes amazing things they are learning about them. All this makes them quite proud and pleased with themselves.

This unanticipated outcome is the greatest payoff for me, and for them, as well. So, please be aware that you are not just writing your life stories for other people, even if that was your original objective. You are doing it for your-self as well. What a great way to spend your "prime-time" years; engaging in an activity that makes you feel good about yourself and your life!

In addition, writing one's autobiography is tremen-dously helpful in keeping the brain and memory func-tioning. You'll find that as you employ *conscious recall* you will *spontaneously remember* incidents and people you hadn't thought of in 30, 40, 50 years, or more. You'll discover that one memory leads to another. You'll be recalling friends and all sorts of things you thought you'd forgotten, and, more than likely, you're going to enjoy the heck out of it.

As you're writing about your life, chances are excel-lent that you will learn a great deal about yourself. The more you write, the more you'll learn. You'll find that patterns will emerge and you'll get some *'Aha!s'* -- rev-elations about yourself, your relationships, and your life.

In addition, writing greatly increases one's powers of observation and communication. You'll find yourself watching and listening closely to whatever's happening around you so that you'll be able to describe things more clearly and completely.

Furthermore, writing one's life experience, especially a not-so-pleasant memory, can be tremendously cathar-tic. It's as if, by getting it down on paper or onto a com-puter disk, you're getting it out of your system -- out of your psyche -- and letting it go. Many a writer has reported this and I have experienced it myself.

In writing about an old trauma or an old enemy, you finally release it, eliminating its power over you. You may find, some time after writing it, that the emotional charge is gone. Finally, it is just another of life's many experiences. Your grief, anger or torment is greatly diminished, if not eliminated.

Even if these stories don't make the final cut and are never seen in your finished work, the emotional result is the same. It's <u>good</u> therapy.

Writing is a form of therapy; sometimes I wonder how all those people who do not write, compose or paint can manage to escape the madness, the melancholia, the panic-fear which is inherent in a human situation.

Graham Greene

"I'LL NEVER DRIVE IN L.A!"

Leta Inlow Fairfield Wright, Fresno, CA

It was World War II. America was fighting on two fronts. There was anguish in our hearts as we watched our young men and women march off to war. Americans at home pulled together in the war effort.

Lawrence got a job designing airplanes at Lockheed so we moved to Southern California. He was exempt from military duty because his job was vital to the war effort. We rented a little house in Burbank, near the Lockheed plant. When we got there and I saw the traffic I swore I'd never drive in Los Angeles. There were so many cars, and drivers were so wild!

As the war went on more of the men went to war. There was a wartime song that went like this: *"They're either too young or too old."* Well, it was right-on. But young or old, everyone did their utmost to help so that our "Yanks" over there would have what they needed.

Remember "Rosie the Riveter"? That's what we women who went to work in the nation's shipyards and aircraft factories were called. I got a job at Lockheed as a welder on the tailpipe assembly of the B-17 Flying Fortress.

I wore a metal face-shield to protect my face and eyes, and we had to wear a cover over our hair. One day a spark hit my turban and ignited my hair. I was not aware of it until my fellow workers starting slapping my head to put out the fire. When it was finally out my group leader made me go right back to work. He said, "If you stop to think about it you'll be afraid to weld again." I admit, it shook me up a little!

I worked at Lockheed until Lawrence was transferred to Phoenix on temporary assignment. That's where Charlie, who was 5, got infantile paralysis. At that time the only thing you could do for polio was the Sister Kenny Treatment: I'd soak pieces of wool blanket in boiling water. Then, picking up one with a stick, I'd put it through the wringer three times to take out the excess water and cool it off enough so it wouldn't scald him. I'd wrap each part of his body in the steaming wool, wrap that in oiled silk, then cover him with a blanket to hold in the heat. By the time one application was finished it was time to start all over again. That's how we spent every day.

After awhile we moved back to Burbank. Once a week Charlie had to go to Children's Hospital in Beverly Hills. I was determined that he would not end up crippled or in an iron lung. So, scared as I was to get on those roads with those crazy drivers, I drove him to Beverly Hills to see the doctors at Children's every week.

When the war was over, we mourned for those who did not return and rejoiced with those who did. We moved back home to Fresno and resumed our peacetime lives.

Charlie had a full recovery. He is a schoolteacher and has given me five beautiful granddaughters.

Writing Activity:

Write a story about your war.

In this book are two stories about the authors' World War II experiences, "I'll Never Drive In L.A." by Leta Wright, and "Crossing the Rhine" by Jackson Clarke, and another which took place during the Korean Conflict, "The Best Meal I Ever Had" by Lawrence Green. Their stories and their writing styles differ greatly but all are excellent personal histories which add to our knowledge of those eras.

Whether you write about WWII, the Korean Conflict, the war in Vietnam or one of the Gulf Wars (or if you lived somewhere other than the U.S., whatever your war was), write about your war experience -- something that occurred; something you did; something someone else did; the mood in the country.

On the following page are some of my recollections of WWII. I was just a kid, so my participation in the war was at a distance. But it's part of my history and it may add to the overall picture of that era.

Write a piece -- a story, an anecdote, a series of recollections -- based on your war experience.

Have fun!

I WAS A KID IN THE WAR YEARS
Carol Petersen Purroy

Fresno was the site of three military bases, so we were very aware of the war and the war effort. My mom and my aunt both volunteered their time and effort after work and on weekends. They helped staff the Lutheran Service Center down on Broadway. Each denomination had a place where servicemen could go to hang out. Coffee, cookies and doughnuts were served, and there was music, pingpong tables and games of all sorts. People of all ages, including kids, went to help out.

Servicemen from The 'Fairgrounds', where Mom had a job in the Motor Pool, were often guests in our home. They'd play the piano, jitterbug with my teenaged cousin Virginia and her girlfriends; we'd make popcorn or fudge, and they'd play Checkers or Old Maid with us kids.

On holidays there'd be as many as we could fit around the table. We'd string together the dining table with the kitchen table and a card table or two, stretching from the dining room all the way through the living room, using chairs borrowed from the neighbors and the piano bench to seat everyone. At Christmas, Mom had some small gift for each one, so they'd have something to open when we were opening our presents.

Rationing was in effect, so we'd save up our rationing stamps for holiday feasts. And many things were in short supply. It was not unusual to see long lines for this thing or that. Nylons were the #1 hot item, but even things

47

like toilet paper caused lines to form.

Franklin Delano Roosevelt was the only president I'd ever known. He'd been president since before I was born. To everyone we knew, he was some sort of a god. Everyone would gather around the radio to listen to his Fireside Chats, hanging on his every word.

On April 12, 1945, I remember this. A girl came into my 4th grade classroom and handed my teacher a note. She signed it and the girl left. Then the teacher sat at her desk and cried. We watched and wondered, but she said nothing. It wasn't until after school let out that we learned what it was all about.

It was at the corner store where we sometimes stopped for a penny candy that we got the news. President Roosevelt was dead!

The nation went into mourning and panic. The war was still on and most doubted that our new president, Harry S. Truman, was capable of leading the country. A great deal of hand-wringing went on. What was to happen to us now?

Then, within a few weeks, the war on both fronts was brought to conclusion. 'Give-'em-hell-Harry' had what it took, after all.

On VE (Victory in Europe) Day (May 8, 1945), and VJ (Victory over Japan) Day (August 15), the whole country exploded with joy and celebration.

YOU'RE THE STAR!

The subject of your memoirs is, of course, you. You are the central character, the star! You are the center of the universe. All the other characters revolve around you as the planets revolve around the sun. All the events of your lifetime exist in relation to you: where you were and what you were doing when they happened; how you felt about and responded to them; how they influenced or affected you; the conflicts or struggles they caused.

When you begin seeing your own life as grist for the literary mill everything changes. You begin to perceive everything as a possible story.

If you're like most people, as you start shining the spotlight on the events and experiences of your life, you'll begin to realize just how fascinating you and your life really are.

SEDUCE YOUR READERS

How do you go about writing a memoir people will want to read? You reach into your bag of tricks (provided throughout this book) and pull them out, one by one, time and again. First and foremost is the fine art of seduction.

Surely you know how to be seductive. You simply promise more that you're willing to deliver at the moment. A woman may coquettishly drop a strap from her shoulder while delivering a smouldering look, then demurely pull it back up . . . . with an unspoken promise in her eyes.

You gotta know, she's got the attention of the object of her seduction. He's positively panting to find out what she will deliver . . . and when. If she's smart, she'll keep him guessing for awhile.

What works in the romantic arena works in the literary one as well. You tease the reader. You make promises for later fulfillment. You drop little hints of things to come.

You allude to the things you'll surrender later -- just enough to lead your reader on -- then sidestep the issue, for now, moving onto something else. In other words, you play hard-to-get.

You tease, entice, allure, tantalize. You lead your readers down the primrose path. You do what is necessary to keep them lusting for more.

In your relationship with your readers, as in any relationship, you don't want to give away too much too soon, or you'll run the risk of losing the relationship. The reader will lose interest if you're "too easy" -- if you give everything away up front.

So, go ahead, be seductive. Make promises, promises . . . holding back, keeping something in reserve.

But please, before it's over, make good on your promises.

SPICE UP YOUR LIFE!

Here's the bag of tricks I promised: strategies for spicing up your life stories and keeping your readers turning those pages.

As I'm sure you're aware, there's always more than one way to say anything. You can write a story in such a way that it is bland as milktoast or you can make it a tangy jambalaya. As you're writing your life stories and painting the scenes of your life with sufficient detail so that your reader can experience them along with you, here are some tricks you can pull out of your hat to spice up your stories:

Incongruities & Paradoxes = Mystery & Intrigue

From time to time, whenever possible, draw readers in with a bit of mystery; a touch of intrigue. Write your introduction to a section, chapter or vignette in such a way that there are incongruities designed to pique the readers' curiosity, causing them to ask, "What is wrong with this picture?", making them wonder, "Why is this person (or thing) out of place; out of sync? What is going on here?"

This is bound to keep your readers flipping pages in order to solve the mystery. The following is such a paradox:

A Bizarre Ritual

Despite the warmth of the summer evening, an icy shiver went through me as I crouched behind the ancient tombstone, making myself as small as I could get. A ghostly moan hung over the graveyard, raising goose-pimples on my bare arms. I gave no thought to my formal gown or the gardenia pinned to it.

Pressing against the rough granite gravemarker, I held my breath. The earth beneath me vibrated with heavy foot-falls as the boy came nearer, nearer, ever nearer.

(The writer [me] hopes that the reader will wonder why this girl, dressed in a formal gown, is hiding in a graveyard at night; who is after her, and why?

I hope the reader will be sufficiently intrigued to keep reading so as to learn the answers to those questions.

In case you are, here's the rest of the story):

He was so close I could have reached out and touched him, but he didn't see me. He went on past. At last, I started breathing again.

A voice called out from the portico of the mausoleum, across West Belmont. "Carol, you're next!" My heart thumping, my hands cold and clammy, I stood up on trembling legs, smoothed my skirt, and left my hiding place, secure in the knowledge that the call gave me immunity from my stalker.

But across the road at the mausoleum a far greater terror lay in store. I wanted to turn tail and run but didn't dare. I hurried past the headstones, stumbling over the uneven burial plots in the old cemetery. The filmy marquisette of my full skirt caught on something. I gave it a yank and ran on, unwilling to make them wait. I knew that would only make it worse.

Pulling open the heavy doors to the great room, I tiptoed in and sank into a chair at the rear. Up front were two black-lacquered grand pianos, their lids uptilted, flanked by sprays of violet gladiolas left from someone's funeral. A blond girl about my age (10-11), in yellow organdy and black patent MaryJanes, sat at one of the pianos, playing her recital piece. She lost her place and had to start over, a chilling reminder of my own worst nightmare.

I tried to calm myself as I waited my turn, taking deep breaths and exhaling slowly, my hands pressed against my thighs to quell their quivering. The girl finished and with a *Thank God, it's over!*-expression, stood, curtsied, and bolted for the door.

The person responsible for this bizarre ritual, Bessie Anderson-Piano Teacher, stood elegant and formidable in long black crepe, reading from the program. She announced, "Carol Petersen will play *'Barcarolle'* by Jacques Offenbach."

Making my way up the center aisle with all the enthusiasm of the condemned approaching the *guillotine,* I reached the piano and sat down. Positioning my trembling fingers over the keys while my foot stretched for the pedal, I started to play the piece I'd practiced and practiced.

Mrs. Anderson served as organist for most of Fresno's funerals, so she could hold her annual recital in the funeral-parlor-of-her-choice. She always chose this elegant marble mausoleum, which her young students were dying to explore. Off the foyer, to the right, were thick glass doors through which a long marble corridor was visible. Inside the walls were crypts filled with dead people. Then, to the left, through another thick glass door, down another long corridor, was the crematorium where, we were told, huge ovens turned dead bodies into "gritty little piles of ashes".

The adolescents among us regaled us younger kids with visions of ghosts and ghouls, and chanted:

The worms crawl in, the worms crawl out.

The worms play tiddlywinks on your snout . . . ,
accompanied by ghastly, ghostly sound-effects, of course.

Right across the road was Mountain View Cemetery where, between our musical tortures, we played Hide-&-Go-Seek among the tombstones. It was great, spooky fun!

———————————

So you see, once in a while, it's fun to play with a story and tell it in such a way as to hook the reader like a big fish, then reel (it) in. I could have told the story 'straight', and it would have been no more, no less true. But it wouldn't have been as much fun for either the writer or the reader.

Similes, Analogies & Metaphors

The use of a <u>simile</u>, <u>analogy</u> or <u>metaphor</u> can make a passage more descriptive and visual. All three are devices through which writers give their readers images to relate to, presenting a clear and colorful mental picture. They are ways of using similarities, comparisons or representations to spice up your writing. It's not necessary to know which is which, but only to be aware of them as techniques to make your stories more interesting and fun to read.

The following over-simplifications give you the idea:

Similes

A simile compares one thing to another, using **as**:
*Dad came home drunk **as** a sailor on shoreleave.*
Or:
*She was as mean **as** a cornered alley cat.*

Analogies

An analogy is something that is ***like*** another.
*Her smile was **like** a halogen lamp in a coal mine.*
Or:
*That pile of straw felt **like** a feather bed to me.*

Metaphors

A metaphor compares a thing to an unrelated concept with shared characteristics, as if it were that thing, e.g:
*A mighty fortress **is** our God.*
*Her lips **were** ripe, luscious plums.*
*The sky **is** an over-turned bowl.*

In each case, the writer conveys the message that the subject **has** the qualities of the metaphor, (e.g: Our god **is** a mighty fortress, i.e., strong, protective, enduring). Her lips make you think of ripe, luscious plums, therefore, metaphorically, they **are** ripe, luscious plums.

Throw 'em A Curve

Every once in a while, do the unexpected. Throw in an image that will catch your reader off guard. Be unpredictable. The trick is to come up with an image that's out of whack, one that pulls readers up short and makes them think. Try this one:

Jane was as easy as the TV Guide Crossword Puzzle.
Or this one:
"Oh, Trevor, take me!" she panted, her bosom heaving like a college freshman on Dollar-a-Beer Night.

Once in awhile, surprise your readers; startle them a little. As in the above sentences, *double entendre*** delivers a terrific 'curve ball'. When you throw one at your readers, it wakes them up, puts smiles on their faces, and has them wanting more.

— — — — — —

* a word with double meanings, i.e., *easy* and *heaving*. The writer exploited *double entendre* for maximum impact.

— — — — — —

Modifiers

Modifiers are descriptive words or phrases used to <u>define, explain or illustrate</u> what you're talking about. They are another way of spicing up your story. With modifiers you can convey a great deal of information and make your story ever-so-much more interesting.

I'll take this basic sentence, *When I got home from my date my mother met me on the porch,* and modify it. Here are three examples (modifiers bold):

• *When I got home from my **very first** date, my mother met **Sid and** me on the **wisteria-draped front** porch **with warm smiles and cold rootbeers**.*

• *When I got home from my date **at 3:00 a.m., a bit tipsy,** my **uptight** mother, **in her dopey pincurls and ratty old bathrobe**, met me **right there** on the porch, **raving like a lunatic**.*

• *When I got home from my **clandestine** date, my **nearly-hysterical** mother met me on the **dark** porch, **both furious and relieved**.*

Each of these sentences portrays a very different scenario and produces a very different feeling. The basic sentence is the same: *When I got home from my date my mother met me on the porch*. The only difference is the modifiers. Their use sets the mood and describes the setting, the people and their emotions, efficiently relating a huge amount of information, all of which makes for a stronger, more interesting story.

So, rather than just giving the basic facts, spice them up and flesh them out with descriptive, explanatory and illustrative words and phrases (a.k.a. adverbs & adjectives).

Synonyms

Synonyms are words or phrases that mean the same

or nearly the same thing. For example, *fate* and *destiny* are synonyms, as are *mystified* and *bewildered*. The use of synonyms helps you keep from being repetitive and dull. But even more important, it allows you to shade the meaning or mood of a passage and/or make it more specific, thereby making your writing more engaging.

In the second modified sentence on the previous page, the word "tipsy" is used to indicate a level of intoxication. You might try substituting other words which do the same thing to see how they change the meaning and/or the mood of the sentence or reveal the writer's intention (e.g: *drunk, soused, bleary-eyed, snockered, falling-down, pie-eyed, boozed-up).*

One can imagine that a synonym such as "snockered" might have been more accurate, but the writer was attempting to portray herself in a good light, so "tipsy" was the word she chose.

Each word choice may alter the feeling or impression of a sentence ever so slightly, yet ever so importantly.

In the next section ('All Those Fancy Words'), you'll learn where to find all the synonyms you'll ever need or want.

Cliffhangers

One surefire way to keep your readers turning pages is to end a section in a 'cliffhanger'.

When I was a kid there were Saturday afternoon serials at the movies, in which every episode ended with the hero in dire straits, sometimes literally hanging off a cliff by his or her fingernails, with the villain about to stomp on the hero's fingers.

Just as we couldn't wait to get back to the movie palace the following week, so will your readers be eager to find out what happens next.

In other words, don't wrap everything up too neatly or too quickly. Build tension, create suspense, anticipation. Make your readers sweat, wondering what the outcome will be. End your chapter or section at a crucial moment.

Dialogue

Dialogue (conversation) adds spice to your literary soup so don't hesitate to put words in your characters' mouths.

Now, I realize that you may not remember exactly what someone said fifty years ago, or even what was said over this morning's Raisin-Bran. But you remember the gist of the conversation, enough to fill in the gaps. All writers exercise *literary license* to jazz up their stories.

When you write *what* someone said, your stories are far more involving than if you just write *about* what someone said. See which of the following two sentences is more interesting:

My father indicated that I should either get a job or find another place to live.

Or this one:

Dad said, "Get a job or get out!"

I think you'll agree that while the second example delivers the same message as the first, it does so with a lot more pizzazz. You actually get a mental picture of 'Dad' saying it.

Dialogue is also useful to bring out a person's personality and character. For example:

Grandpa said, "I always said Jake was gonna live forever, "cause he's too dang mean to die'."

or:

Grandpa declared, "The world is a far better place because of Jake. With his passing, it is much improved."

Here we have two 'Grandpas' expressing the same sentiment about 'Jake'. Their speech reveals a great deal about them. The first appears to be a cantankerous old guy who 'tells it like it is', while the second seems somewhat philosophical and subtly humorous. That was accomplished merely through the use of dialogue -- by putting words in their mouths.

The writer could have just said, "Grandpa didn't like Jake." But dialogue allows 'Grandpa' to develop into a real person.

Dialogue is one of the most useful tools a writer has for spicing up a story and bringing the characters to life. Use it.

Writing Activity:

Write a story in which you use Paradox or Inconsistency to hook your reader in.

The topic can be anything. If you need help with a story-idea, look through the list in 'What To Write About' on page 10, or the 'Where To Get Ideas' section on page 20.

- ◆ Plant doubt or confusion in your readers' minds. Make them ask "What is wrong with this picture?"

- ◆ Play a trick on your readers. Make them think you're talking about one thing when you're actually going in a whole different direction.

- ◆ Use as many of the other 'Spice Up Your Life' techniques as you can in writing your story.

- ◆ Have fun!

Recollections of grandfather; influential person

WITHOUT A LEG TO STAND ON

Barbara Jordan, orator, 1st Southern Black Congresswoman

. . . John Ed Patten was among those released "on full and unconditional pardon; friendless and penniless," in the language of the law, into custody of his faithful attorney, J. M., Gibson. A free man, he enclosed himself in a fenced business. . . . both a buffer against the world and an eyesore to it.

What future hopes he had he now put on his eldest daughter, Arlyne, a bright girl already beginning to make a name for herself as an orator in the Baptist church. As she grew up he encouraged her, built up her command of English, shaped her flare and fire with his inflections and intonations. Then she, too, was lost to him.

Eschewing her considerable gifts, she chose instead to secure the middle-class respectable family life of which his prison term robbed her. She married . . .

Outraged, robbed again of promise, John Ed refused to attend his daughter's wedding. Instead, he . . . watched her turn her full attention to being Ben's subservient wife, and the mother, in four years, of three daughters.

Barbara Charline, born February 21, 1936, was nurtured and welcomed by her mother; . . . her father, on the other hand, looked at this third female, coal black and glistening, and asked, "Why is she so dark?"

This obstreperous infant's immediate response gave John Ed one last chance. By the time she was ten months old he carried around a snapshot of her marked, *MY HEART.*

He read to her in the front bedroom of the frame house at Webster and Matthew streets; . . . read to an attentive, skinny, long-legged five-year-old, with hair in tight plaits, her face fastened on his; read rocking back and forth in an old chair stuffed with cushions, peering over his dime-store reading glasses, by the light of a kerosene lantern, from a worn volume of *Songs of the Blood Washed.*

. . . He read from *The King James Bible* and from *Saalfield's Standard Vest Pocket Pronouncing Dictionary.* He talked to her as a teacher to a student . . . and as an aging man to what had become the idol of his life -- allowing him to become the foundation, the cornerstone, of hers.

In time, when she was at college, set on a path of becoming the Washington lawyer of the new generation, he found no further use for himself. One evening, drunk on wine, wandering aimlessly, he stumbled on the railroad tracks and was hit by a train, which severed both his legs at the hips.

"Don't let Barbara see me," he begged Arlyne.

"What are you doing here?" he asked his favorite when she arrived at Jeff Davis Hospital to stare down at the spot where the sheet dropped flat. Seeing her one last time, he gave up and died, abdicating a world which had left him without a leg to stand on.

Note: The author chose to write her autobiography in the 3rd person, using 'she' and 'her' in reference to herself.

ALL THOSE FANCY WORDS

I often hear, "I can't write. I don't know all those fancy words!"

Relax. You don't need to know a lot of fancy words. Some of the most endearing and enduring literature is written with common, ordinary, garden-variety words.

Take *The Adventures of Tom Sawyer*, by Mark Twain. Are there any words in it you couldn't have written? (Well, maybe a few, but that's because it was written in the 19th century and uses words we now consider 'quaint'.)

Part of the reason it is so well-loved and wears so well is that it is simply written. It doesn't try to impress anyone with a lot of four-bit words. It tells the story of a 10-year-old boy who lived in a small Midwestern town in the mid-19th-century. Although Samuel Clemens (Mark Twain) had a 'fancy' vocabulary, he chose to tell this story plainly. And because it is the story of plain folks in a plain town, telling it that way makes it all the more powerful.

As a writer, however, you want to keep your story interesting, so you won't want to use the same word over and over and over (except where you need to for emphasis or to make a point, as I just did).

The best writers' aid I've found is *The Synonym Finder* (J. I. Rodale, Rodale Press, Emmaus, PA, 1978). You just look up the word you're thinking of and it provides more synonyms than you'll ever need.

For example, you may need a synonym for **tension**. I chose it because it is one of the shorter selections.

tension, *n. 1. tautness, tightness, extension, distension, elongation; pull, tug, yank, strain; stretch, draw, traction, tensity.*
2. anxiety, uneasiness, disquiet, disquietude, inquietude, fretfulness; worry, trouble, concern, vexation; pressure, stress, heat, burden, cross, encumbrance, cumbrance, nervousness, ants. Inf. *butterflies.* Sl. *habdabs; excitement, agitation, perturbation, suspense, anticipation, expectation, apprehension, fear.*

Among the synonyms listed, you're sure to find one that will work for you.

While a good dictionary is essential, it's my *Synonym Finder* that gets the most use. I've worn out two copies, so far, and the third is ready to fall apart. Most bookstores have it in stock or will be happy to order it for you.

As you write you'll probably notice that your vocabulary increases. You may even discover that words can be fun. You may start making a mental note or jotting down a word or phrase when you hear one that is especially powerful or descriptive or appropriate to your story.

Recollections of World War II

CROSSING THE RHINE

Jackson C. Clarke, San Andreas

We got to the Rhine River . . . we had to cross (it) to get on to Berlin. When we arrived . . . we stopped and went into position; the guns in the firing position.

That afternoon, we saw a Jeep with four guys in it. The three passengers were General Eisenhower, General Bradley, and Churchill. It turned out that they were inspecting the troops just prior to the crossing of the Rhine River.

I was called in by the Intelligence Officer, Captain Earl . . . He called me up to the battalion headquarters and said, "Jack, the colonel wants you to go out as the Forward Observer. I want to brief you on what to expect. Oh, incidentally, Clarke, I think you might find this handy," and he handed me a Thompson submachine gun . . .

"If you need it and have to start firing, don't fire more than half-a-dozen rounds with one burst, because if you do, it'll pull the point of the gun up into the air. . . . Just fire a short burst, then pause and pull the gun down and fire another burst."

So I kind of chuckled. *Well, okay.*

Then, he also advised me that . . . the shore over on the other side, where we were supposed to land, was full of antipersonnel mines . . .

"Well, okay," I said. "I guess we'll have to cope. . ."

He told me what time to report -- after dark -- to the infantry company I would be accompanying . . . The

Germans seemed to know that we were going to attempt to cross the Rhine that night, and they opened up.

... Starting about 10 o'clock, the heavy firing began. I've seen many Fourth of July fireworks but I have never seen one that equaled the fireworks when we crossed the Rhine. It was completely spectacular. From horizon to horizon the air was full of tracers, explosions, plus anti-aircraft fire. The Germans were firing everything they could ... And, of course, our artillery and machine guns were firing right back just as heavily, maybe heavier.

The sky was absolutely full of fireworks. It was an amazing sight, a really amazing sight!

In any event, I joined the company ... we were scheduled to cross at 3:30 a.m. ... So we went and found the boat we were going to cross on. It was ... more like a rowboat than anything else, with an outboard motor on the back end. And a Sailor operating the boat. When I saw this guy in a sailor's uniform, sitting there at the backend of the damn boat, at the outboard motor, I said, "What's he doing here?"

"Well, it's a boat, so it's a Navy operation!" ...

In any event, we crossed the Rhine in this little rowboat. It held six people. ... There were these same-sized rowboats all alongside each other, all these G.I.s were in the other boats, coming across. The Rhine seemed like it was about 10 miles wide, it took so long to get across.

... Well, we landed on the other side and I kept waiting for the anti-personnel mines to go off, but none did. So, apparently, the intelligence was not accurate.

Thank heavens!

ORGANIZING YOUR AUTOBIOGRAPHY

Chronological Order

There are many ways to organize your autobiography. There is, of course, the old standard, tried-and-true chronological order, starting at your birth (or an earlier time, if you're including your family's history), and moving through time.

There's a lot to be said for this order of things. It does provide a structural framework on which to build your story. And it can be combined with any number of styles and forms.

It is not without peril, though. The danger is that you may be tempted to simply note the events of your life chronologically (e.g: I was born in Poughkeepsie in 1934; I started Kindergarten in 1939; in 1944 I got a two-wheel bike; I moved to Detroit in 1951 and got my first Ford; in 1952 I graduated and joined the Navy; I enrolled at Michigan State in 1956 . . .)

Never, *never, NEVER* do that! That's a laundry list. And it's a real 'yawner'. It tells nothing about you, nor does it make the reader want to know about you -- even those who love you! I suppose it's better than nothing, but not much! What it tells the reader is, "This person is a colossal bore!" Now, you and I both know you're not, but you sure couldn't tell it from that.

There are many things you can do to avoid the 'laundry list' approach to autobiography. For one thing, instead of saying, "I was born on . . ." tell a story about it, e.g:

"The night before I was born, 'The Great Blizzard of '38' came through. Early next morning, Dad and Grandad shoveled snow, 6'-deep, all the way to the main road, about 100 yards, so Doc Hammil could get his Model-T up to 28 Gooseberry Lane and give Mom a hand."

Or: "My parents hadn't even thought about boys names. They *knew* I was going to be a girl. They kept blaming each other for having a another boy and fighting about it, so after 2 weeks, I still didn't have a name. Grandma lost patience with them and made out the birth certificate herself. She named me for her movie idol, Rudolf Valentino."

As you've seen, throughout this book are ways to show your reader how interesting you and your life are; devices through which to breathe life into them, to transport your readers into a scene, to elicit their emotions, to make them want to know more about you. Read on.

By Theme

What's your passion? What is there that has been a constant throughout most of your life? You may decide to write your stories according to a theme, choosing a thread that runs through your life and using it to tie your stories together. For instance:

• **Career:** You may want to make your career a major character in your story, telling how it has taken you through life, or, if you've changed careers, how your career choices came about and how they have impacted your life. You may want to draw a parallel between your personal growth and your career advancement.

• **Animals:** Perhaps you're an animal lover. Your story would be incomplete without the pets or wild animals that have been part of your life.

• **Adventure:** Maybe you're an adventurer. Your life story will certainly be about your grand adventures because that's who you are. Your adventures tell their own tale.

• **Parties, social events:** If you're the "host or hostess with the mostest," you may want to tell your life story by relating the great parties you've thrown. You may want to include guest lists, food served, decorations, etc. And you'll definitely want to talk about the function of an event -- its purpose or reason for being.

• **Clothes:** Do you love clothes? Your theme could involve the outfit or ensemble you were wearing for each of the important events of your life, perhaps with photos or sketches of them.

• **Cars:** Are cars your passion? You may relate the events of your life to the car you were driving when they occurred.

• **Airplanes:** Did you experience "love at first flight?" If so, write about the planes and flights of your life, where they took you; your flying adventures.

• **Films:** If you're a movie buff you could relate your life's events to the movies and movie stars of your life, including insights on how they influenced you.

• **Sports:** Is sports in general, or a specific sport, your passion? That then may be the thread that runs through your life stories.

• ~~**Disability**~~**:** Did/do you have what society deems a "disability?" Your readers will want to know about the challenges you've faced and how you've dealt with them. They'll want to know how your disability has affected your life, how it has (or has not) defined you, and your reflections on it.

• **Minority:** Are you a member of a racial, ethnic, religious, gender or sexual-orientation group towards which society's attitude and laws have changed in your lifetime? Your theme could well be the societal changes and relevant turning-points you have witnessed or participated in, or the discrimination you've experienced, what it's done to you, and what you've felt and done about it.

• **Collectibles**: If you're a collector, talk about your collection(s). As you write about each piece, you'll be telling about yourself; about your stage in life, where you were and what you were doing, what you were thinking and feeling as each item became part of your collection.

• **Music**: Music is an enormous part of life for many of us. You can write your story in terms of the music that touched you at each step along the way.

Play with the idea. The bottom line is, it's your life and your life story. Make it truly yours by telling about the things that matter to you. Let your readers in on who you are and what you care about. Give them indications of what it (your theme-topic) has meant to you and how it has affected your life. It will give them real insights into you.

You'll see, as you're writing, that just about any theme will work. And as you write about your theme you can place it in the personal and worldwide events of your lifetime.

Comparative

One of the results of having lived a long time is that we have acquired a unique frame of reference or perspective. We've lived in the most amazing period in all of history. The last 100 years have seen the first manned flight, the first transoceanic flight, the first jet airplane, spaceships, men walking on the moon, and (as this goes to print), spaceships landing on Mars, photographing Venus.

A short 100 years ago, at the turn of the 20th century, very few households had electricity or indoor plumbing, a telephone or an automobile. Many of the things we take for granted were then the stuff of science fiction. Now that we are in the 21st century, the majority of homes in America has at least one computer with instantaneous worldwide internet access, a stereophonic or multiphonic sound system, electronic games, and cellular phones.

We have truly gone from "a glimpse of stocking" as *shocking,* to "anything goes." We now accept full nudity and steamy sex scenes in movies and even on TV sitcoms. We've gone from a time when a relatively mild profanity ("Frankly, my dear, I don't give a damn!") nearly blocked the release of a spectacular film, to the point, now, where every second word in some movies is . . . well, you know. It's no longer considered shocking. "Anything goes" is a fact of modern life.

Much less than 100 years ago in the U.S., social, political, economic and legal discrimination against non-males, non-Christians, non-heterosexuals, and persons of non-European descent was the norm, sanctioned by law and accepted by society in general. Now, while it hasn't totally disappeared, such discrimination is at least generally illegal. Our 'collective consciousness' has raised to the point where it's no longer acceptable to the majority.

Having lived through this, we have achieved a perspective which enables us to discuss our earlier actions, attitudes and customs, on both a personal and societal level, and report on the changes. We're able to compare our former selves with our present selves, previous times with the present, prior biases and prejudices with current attitudes, former mores with current ones, and tell how those changes have affected our lives.

Personal Essays

If writing your memoirs, *per se,* doesn't appeal to you, there are other options, such as personal essays -- 'think pieces' -- your opinions about anything and everything.

The great 19th-century American essayist, Ralph Waldo Emerson, never wrote an autobiography, yet we know a great deal about him through his essays. He left a rich and varied legacy that gives readers tremendous insight into the era in which he lived, what he thought about a great many things, how he felt about the issues of the day, as well as his viewpoint on the great philosophical quandaries of the ages.

And what about Erma Bombeck? We felt as if we knew her, almost as if she were a member of our family or a dear coffee-klatch neighbor. Personal essays were her forte. She just wrote about common, ordinary, everyday things: kids, husband, PTA meetings, the family car, the family dog, the family septic tank, things we could relate to. A great many of us felt so close to her that we mourned her death. That was because she had shared herself with us through her essays.

So, rather than get involved in writing the *stories* of your life, you may wish to write your thoughts, feelings and emotions about all kinds of things! Pretend you're a newspaper or magazine columnist: pick a topic a week and explore it in writing.

This could be your legacy. And what a wonderful legacy it will be!

The Combination Plate

The combination of any or all of the above ways of creating your legacy is perfectly acceptable. If you are writing your memoirs, you may wish to include an occasional 'think piece' among your life stories and recollections. It will help round out the picture of you for your readers.

Remember, this is *your* creation and it can be as unique as you are.

Writing Activity:

Write a story in which a vehicle (car, truck, plane, train or boat) played a part.

◆ Be sure to tell (if appropriate):
- How/when it came into your life.
- What it looked like; the make, model & year.
- What was unique or unusual about it.
- How you felt about it -- what it meant to you.
- How you felt when you operated it.
- An adventure (or several) related to it.
- Any trouble or conflict it caused you.

On the following pages are two stories involving a car, as examples. One is from the male point of view, the other, the female* -- altogether different, as you'll be quick to notice.

* Actually, I wrote 'In My Boyfriend's 1941 Ford' to show how a piece of music can trigger a memory and inspire a story, but it's about a car, too, so it works for this Writing Activity, as well.

Cars, recollections of a parent.

"DO IT AGAIN!"

Ronald V. Allen, Reno, NV

Pa bought a GMC truck for hauling wood. The truck was unusual because it had no battery. It wasn't missing; it hadn't been equipped with one. It had large magneto coils and had to be started by hand-cranking. It was a 4-cylinder. I remember the putt-putt sound it made.

On very cold mornings Pa would get the truck running and then help the neighbors jumpstart their cars.

Anyway, Pa got a 3 X 8' piece of sheet steel, which he bolted onto the front of the GMC for a snowplow. Since the sheet was flat, the angle of the plow would not curl the snow off to the side as snowplows do. Instead, the force of the snow would cause the truck to slide off to one side when Pa hit the snowbank. That didn't stop him.

"We need more weight in the truck," he'd say. All the kids in the neighborhood jumped in the back. Pa then backed up the truck and made a run at the snow. When the flat sheet of steel smashed against the snow; a gorgeous white plume shot 20-feet straight up in the air. He was having the time of his life, and so were we.

"Do it again!" we yelled. "Do it again!"

"Hang on!" he yelled back, and we waited for the resounding boom and the snow flying into the sky. He battered his way to Washington Street with all of us hanging on for dear life, beside ourselves with the joy of participating in Pa Allen's most magnificent experiment.

AUTOBIOGRAPHICAL EXCERPT

Music; Cars; First love

IN MY BOYFRIEND'S 1941 FORD

Carol Petersen Purroy, Reno, NV

Whenever I hear a particular Nat King Cole recording, I'm transported back in time. Once again, I'm in the passenger seat of my boyfriend's 1941 white Ford coupe. We're parked at the curb in front of my house after a city league softball game in which he played shortstop. On the way home we'd stopped, along with the rest of the team and its cheering section, at Stan's Drive-In for a coke. I'm reluctant to say goodnight and go inside. He's in no great hurry either.

The radio's on. It's a hot summer night so the windows are open. The scent of the big old sycamores along the street mingles with his Old Spice and shortstop-sweat. I'm in heaven! I'm 17 and he's 20; we're each other's first love.

At his urging, I scooch across the seat 'til we're touching. His arm comes 'round my shoulders. He takes off his horn-rimmed glasses and places them on the dashboard. I remove my retainer, wrap it in a hankie and set it in my lap. These preparations complete, we turn toward each other. I lift my lips to his. I'm feeling flushed and my heart's all a-flutter.

From the radio the satiny voice of Nat Cole croons,
They tried to tell us we're too young,
Too young to really be in love . . .
. . . And then, someday, they may recall,
We were not too young at all.

Although we've been going steady for almost a year we're still very innocent, due in part to the caring efforts of my across-the-street neighbor, Mrs. 'H'.

(Since my mother's death the previous July, Mrs. 'H' has appointed herself a sort-of guardian. Whenever we'd drive up out front after a date, whatever the hour, she'd give us about ten minutes. Then all her outside lights would come on and she'd step out onto her front porch. Watering can in hand, she'd tend to her geraniums! If she ran out of water before we were ready to call it a night she'd nonchalantly pick dead leaves and blossoms until we were.)

Tonight, since it is summer, she's wearing only a nightgown, a long chartreuse nylon jersey gown. The porch light behind her displays her ample silhouette through the filmy nightie. As she bends over the flowerboxes her plentiful bosom all but overflows.

By this time we're laughing so hard our romantic mood is broken. Illuminating his gold Bulova with his Zippo lighter, he sighs, shrugs, puts on his glasses and comes around to open my door. I take his hand and step out. There's a crunch underfoot. I've stepped on my retainer. Again. "Damn!" I swear under my breath.

At the front door he kisses me goodnight. Mrs. 'H' has turned away but her presence is still felt. I step inside the dimly lit living room and close the door behind me, singing softly, *". . . And then, someday, they may recall, We were not too young at all."*

HOW TO EAT AN ELEPHANT

Do you feel daunted by the fact that there's so much to write about or that there are so many options regarding writing it? How on earth are you supposed to write about your life?

It's like the old riddle, *How do you eat an elephant?* The answer, is, of course, *One bite at a time.* One sentence at a time. One scene at a time. One event at a time. One unforgettable character at a time.

The bag of tricks I gave you earlier to spice up your memoirs will make them more interesting and exciting. But right now, I'm urging you to just get started. Just start writing. Just get your recollections on paper or computer disk. You can go back later and spice them up. You can fill in the gaps and the details later. And you can tighten up your work when you're nearly done.

It's important that you do so, but to get started, just get started. Just start writing.

Rewriting

It's been said that great novels are not written; they are *rewritten*. The same is true of good memoirs. You will no doubt want, at some point, to make corrections, additions and deletions to your first draft. Ultimately, you will have a really good finished product. But don't feel that you must write it in its finished form the first time through. All writers rewrite and revise.

> *I have written, often several times, every word I have ever published. My pencils outlast their erasers.*
>
> Vladimir Nobokov

To get started you must get *something* in writing. You can't change something that doesn't exist. As long as it's just an idea floating around in your head, no matter how great an idea it is, there's nothing of substance to work with. So get your idea, your basic story, down on paper. Then you can go back and change it, adding wonderful details and descriptions, removing the redundant or superfluous, all of which will help make it *really good*.

As you do so, you will see it growing into something you'll be proud of. And you will see yourself growing into a writer, a real writer, with your own style and flair.

Unless you have a publishing house making the decisions on your work, you are the one who decides when a story, chapter or segment is done. You may do as little or as much rewriting as you feel comfortable with.

As you're writing, editing and rewriting, all the while developing your own style, you'll appreciate all the help you can get. The beauty of modern technology (computers), is that you needn't feel that whatever you write is carved in Mt. Rushmore. It's simple to change whatever you have written. You can readily make corrections, move paragraphs or chapters willy-nilly, take the beginning and make it the end, and insert or delete a word, sentence or chapter whenever and wherever you want to.

I recommend becoming computer-literate for this project if you haven't already done so. Many extremely mature adults have and it has changed and enriched their lives. Along with a computer for the actual writing of it, a scanner and color printer will enable you to include photographs and other memorabilia which will enhance your finished edition.

However, as you know, people have been writing without benefit of computers, scanners and color printers for centuries and have created great works. So don't let the fact that you have no computer or computer skills stop you. While a computer does make it easier, it's not essential. It matters not whether you write on a yellow legal pad, a typewriter, or the newest, zingiest computer.

In short, don't place obstacles in your way. Just get started and just do it.

One bite at a time.

Household item; Furniture; Movies

ALMOST A MEMBER OF THE FAMILY

Carol Petersen Purroy, Reno, NV

I'd always wanted a grandfather clock, I don't know why. It may go back to the movies of my childhood in which families of substance always had one. It may have seemed to me that a grandfather clock in your home meant you were **Somebody**.

Both John and I sprang from working-class families in which 'Necessities-Only' was the rule. A grandfather clock was hardly a necessity and he wouldn't hear of it.

Then one day in 1971, I heard about this guy, "J," who had brought a whole slew of antique clocks from Europe and was selling them at bargain prices.

"Can we get one?" I asked John. His reply, as expected, was, "No. Absolutely not!" He had all the usual reasons. "We can't afford it." "Where would we put it?" and "Things like that are for rich people, not people like us."

I would not be dissuaded. "We could at least go *look*, and *see* if we can afford one." "We can put it in the entry hall." And, "**We** deserve to have nice things, too."

Then he hit me with this one: "A grandfather clock is top-heavy. It'll fall over and kill one of the children."

I guffawed. He had the good grace to look sheepish.

"I **really** want a grandfather clock. I've **always** wanted a grandfather clock. We can bolt it to the wall if it'll make you feel any better. . . . . **Please!**"

He relented. I could go look, but he set a limit of $200

When I went to look at the clocks "J" wasn't home so his wife took me out to the barn where there were 75 clocks, maybe more. How to choose? Many were eliminated by my $200 limit, but one was in my price range. She said it was $150. It was one of the smaller, plainer ones. *That's probably why it's so cheap,* I thought. "I'll take it," I said.

Then "J" drove up and came into the barn. When his wife told him of our transaction he looked stricken. "No," he declared. "That's a *really* good clock, worth a lot more."

"But," I insisted, "she **said** I could have it for $150."

He shook his head. "It's one of my best clocks. Besides, somebody already put a deposit on it." He seemed to waver. "But . . . that *was* a month ago and . . . she *hasn't* come back for it. Tell you what, you can have it for $350."

"I only have $200."

He sighed, staring at his shoes, then grimaced. "Okay. $200." He then told me about the woman who had put the deposit on it. "She brought a tape measure and measured all its dimensions. She was going to use it for her ***coffin!*** So *(sigh)* if you want it, you can have it."

He delivered it and set it up in our entry hall, the very center of the house. "Keep it level, polish it weekly, and enjoy it." We have.

It is the heartbeat of my home, its pendulum swinging steadily, rhythmically, day in and day out; its chime, mellow and melodious, pealing on the hour and the half-hour. And it is lovely, a pleasure to look at. It quickly became almost a member of the family, standing there just inside the front door, a loving 'grandfather' welcoming us all home from our wanderings.

Writing Activity:

Write about an object, an item, a thing.

◆ Pick something you'd like to write about, something you own, once owned or aspired to own, something your family owned:

  ● A piece of furniture, jewelry, china, silver, clothing, a toy, car, boat or plane, a collectible, a house or piece of property -- it could be anything.

◆ Write about:

  ● what you know of its history.

  ● what is unique or special about it.

  ● how/when it came into your (or your family's) possession, if it did.

  ● what it means or meant to you (and/or your family), and why.

  ● special occasions you associate with it, if any.

  ● the people you associate with it, if any.

◆ Have fun!

BE NATURAL

> *You can be a little ungrammatical*
> *if you come from the right part*
> *of the country.*
>
> Robert Frost

Don't be afraid to be your own natural self. You want your reader to know who you are, so don't leave out the colorful speech patterns, the colloquialisms and dialect, the quaint or quirky expressions used in your part of the country or by you and your family.

The following is an example of writing naturally, from Freddie Mae Baxter's autobiography, *The Seventh Child: A Lucky Life:*

When I was growing up, you better not say anything about sex. You didn't ask no questions then. You didn't ask, "Momma, how do you get to be a momma?" or "Momma, where do babies come from?" You couldn't ask those kind of questions. . . . In those days, when we started getting a little sassy around the pants, they'd say, "Keep your dress down . . ." But they didn't want to tell you why we should keep our dress down. You couldn't ask.

Notice how you get a real feel for this person because she writes as she speaks. And the phrase, . . . *a little sassy around the pants . . . ,* is so expressive I couldn't help visualizing that sassy little girl swaying her little hips and swishing her little skirt in that flirty way little girls do.

With that charming colloquialism, Freddie Mae Baxter creates a picture in her reader's mind worth a whole lot of words.

> *A man who writes well writes not as others write, as he himself writes; it is often in speaking badly that he speaks well.*
>
> Montesquieu

Your memoir is an extension of you. Through it people will get to know you, so write the way you speak.

Ernest Hemingway said this of his writing style:

In stating as fully as I could how things really were, it was very difficult and I wrote awkwardly and the awkwardness is what they called my style. All mistakes and awkwardness are easy to see, and they called it <u>style</u>.

On the following page is an excerpt from Will James' book, *Lone Cowboy*. It is a fine example of writing naturally.

AUTOBIOGRAPHICAL EXCERPT

<u>*Writing naturally; How values were taught*</u>

THE FIRST TOWN I'D EVER SEEN

Will James

One day in our ramblings through that country we run acrost a whole town, the first town I'd ever seen, and it was deserted. . . . but I got a big thrill looking thru it. I'd never seen such big houses as was there, two and three floors high, and whole rows of 'em with no space between. . . . Some was made out of brick and stone, with big high steel shutters on the windows, and steel doors. I wondered what was inside of them.

In the houses I could get into I found enough things new and of interest to keep me exploring forever, I thought. There was fancy chairs and bedsteads, bureaus and dressers with some clothes still in 'em, pictures on the wall, and everything that's in any home where folks live steady, from the top story down to the cellar.

In some places there was pianos and pump organs. Bopy made me acquainted with them music boxes and for awhile I had a lot of fun making noise. But I never was cut out to handle music, so after awhile, I went on exploring some more. I was looking for the big houses now, with the fancy front porch, because them always had good pictures on the walls inside, and the part of town where the shacks was didn't interest me no more.

We picketed or hobbled our ponies on the streets in that town. The grass had growed tall there and many a blade and bunch of it edged through the cracks of the board sidewalk. I'd got to know the town pretty well in a short while and I'd picked up quite a few things and stacked 'em at camp so I could take 'em along when we moved. But soon as Bopy found that out he made me take 'em all back and put 'em exactly where I'd found 'em. He said something about good men never taking things that don't belong to them.

And so, as much as I hated to, I took everything back, all but two old rusty spurs which I'd found while I was rummaging around the livery stable. They wasn't even mates, but the way I begged Bopy to let me keep them I guess he thought they was sure worth everything to me. I finally got his consent.

Lone Cowboy, Scribner & Sons, New York, NY. 1930

THE QUESTIONS YOU MUST ANSWER

Who, What, When, Where & Why are known as 'The Five W's of Writing'. They are the questions which must be answered in every story. This is the first lesson Journalism students learn. The answers to these questions are what make their story. These questions must be addressed or there's no story. The reader needs to know:

Who the story is about. In most cases, for you autobiographers, it is you. But there are probably other people in your stories, too. You need to let the reader know just who you are and who those other people are.

What the story is about: its subject matter.

Where your story takes place: the setting.

When the story takes place: the timeframe.

Why you wrote the story: the point.

(I'm going to add a 6th 'W of Writing': **HOW**. [Hold it up to a mirror!])

How the story unfolds: how goals are accomplished; how things get done, how the hero's transformation occurs.

We'll discuss these more later.

CONTEXT

Context is simply the time and place -- the 'where and when' -- in which a story occurs, two of the questions that must be answered. Placing your life's adventures in context gives them added authenticity and credibility.

It's a good idea to weave into your stories the events of the day; the songs, movies, cars, toys, radio/TV shows, styles and fashions, fads, hairstyles, appliances; celebrities and politicians; as well as landmarks to identify the place(s) in which the story occurs.

Some of it you may remember, like where you were when you learned that JFK was shot or what song topped 'The Hit Parade' the week of your senior prom). Those are the easy things. There are plenty of other things you'll want to include -- details that will make your story more engaging and help people relate to it -- but most of us need a little help remembering them.

A little research will help refresh your memory. There are several very helpful resources at your disposal:

◆ **20th Century Retrospectives**: At the turn of the 21st Century, several publications came out chronicling the events of the 20th Century, year-by-year and week-by-week. Each is a treasure-trove.

An old **catalog** such as *Sears & Roebuck* will provide all manner of references for your stories. It inspired the piece I wrote about my grandmother's stereopticon (page 133). Some of these old catalogs have recently been reissued in commemorative editions.

◆ Your **local library**. More than likely, your library has copies of old newspapers, catalogs and magazines, dating all the way back to day-one, stored on *microfiche.*

◆ Your town's **historical society** is a great resource. It can supply the details that will lend authority and local tidbits to your life stories. If you no longer live in the town you're writing about, it's still your best bet. If possible, go there and pay a visit to the historical society. And while you're there, try to establish a relationship with someone who works there. Then, when you leave, you'll have a friendly, helpful connection with whom you can stay in touch by phone or email to get your questions answered. They'll also answer your questions and even provide old photos if you contact them by phone or on the internet.

The following is an excerpt from one of my stories. To refresh my memory regarding the two weeks covered in the piece, I looked it up in one of the 20th Century retrospective publications. The information I found there enabled me to better establish the context.

The Original Ship of Fools

It was mid-winter 1956. We were returning from a year-

and-a-half in Germany. John was a lowly 'Spec 3' -- a draftee -- on Cold War duty, and I had tagged along. We had embarked in Bremerhaven and crossed the endless expanse of the North Atlantic Sea toward a port in New Jersey.

. . . Because I was with him, John was allowed to come up to the ship's Common Room for part of the day. Enlisted men traveling without family had to stay in the hot, airless hold which, John reported, was pretty putrid. In the center of the room a garbage can stood, with guys shoving each other out of the way so they could throw up in it.

I, on the other hand, four months pregnant with morning sickness the norm, was surprised by my healthy appetite and lack of nausea on this rough crossing. A lot of passengers didn't even make it to the dining room.

. . . We'd left Germany just after the Hungarian uprising and had been concerned that we'd be held up by it. All the men aboard this olive-drab Army ship had been poised to go to Hungary to do battle had our government kept its promise to the anti-Communist Freedom Fighters. But it hadn't.

. . . Out there, in the middle of the ocean, we were hungry for news. In addition to the Hungarian revolution, Eisenhower and Nixon had just been reelected, which probably meant *status quo*, but you never know. The guys wanted news of college and pro football games. Elvis Presley was hotter than hot; any news of him was bound to be titillating. And movie star Grace Kelly had recently married Monaco's Prince Rainier; we women were eager for news of the fairytale couple.

A few days out there was a news bulletin of sorts, passed by word-of-mouth: Elvis Presley had died! That's all: no details. Just, Elvis was dead! Word of it spread through the ship with the speed of light. The news was alarming, in part, because he was one of us. Elvis and I, and probably half the people on that ship, were just 21 years old. Too young to die. There was a great deal of speculation as to the how, when and where of it.

. . . We rolled on, one icy storm after another, one game of **Parchesi** after another, one long, boring day after another. Interspersed were reminiscences of 'The King' and his songs: *Heartbreak Hotel, You Ain't Nuthin' But A Hound Dog, Love Me Tender, Blue Suede Shoes.*

One day, we were thrilled when another ship passed by. Everyone who could get out on deck did. We waved and hollered to the passengers on the other vessel, who waved and hollered back, while the ships whistled and tooted at one another.

We were not thrilled, however, that the passing ship was going in the same direction we were.

. . . Finally, the interminable voyage was nearing its end. As the Statue of Liberty came into view, the officer who had circulated the story of Elvis' untimely death saw fit to reveal the rest of the story:

"Elvis had a heart attack and died," he solemnly intoned, " . . . . when his hound dog shit on his blue suede shoes!"

Oh no! We'd been duped. We'd swallowed the bogus news story hook, line & sinker. Ours was the original ship of fools!

. . . And we all had a good laugh out of it.

You can see how, by mentioning current events, songs and celebrities of the day, along with cities, a well-known landmark, and the vast ocean to indicate location, the story's context is set. The reader gets a feeling for its time and place.

Now let's take a look at this story in terms of the 'W's of Writing'. Let's see how those questions are answered:

Who?: John and I.

What?: A voyage on an Army ship (whoever heard of such a thing?).

When?: Winter of 1956.

Where?: Crossing the North Atlantic from Bremerhaven, then entering New York harbor to a New Jersey port.

Why?: This anecdote tells about an episode in the writer's life in which boredom, gossip and gullibility play a part. It reveals something about the Cold War Era and the early days of Rock & Roll.

How?: The boredom of the passengers was relieved by an officer's creative distraction; it shows the mode of travel by which they got from Europe to the U.S.; how seasickness was handled on a less-than-luxury ocean liner.

*I'll be 80
this month. Age,
if nothing else, entitles
me to set the record straight
before I dissolve. I've given my
memoirs far more thought
than any of my marriages.
You can't divorce
a book.*

Gloria Swanson

LIFE PATTERNS

One of the many advantages of living a long life is that we can notice patterns, repetitive behaviors, and begin to make some sense out of them. From the vantage point of your present self, you may be able to look back and discern one or more of the patterns in your life. One of them may provide the jumping-off point for your memoir and the framework for it. Discussing a life pattern will allow you to become a bit introspective, which is not a bad thing in autobiographic writing.

There is at least one consistent pattern in my life. The following discussion of it will be the *Preface* for my memoirs.

My mother used to say, "Carol can do anything she wants to. She just doesn't want to do very much."

Little did she know. The truth is, I want to do it all. I want to do everything, go everywhere, learn everything, experience everything, be everything! Everything that interests me, that is. And a lot of things interest me.

Part of what my mom saw when I was a kid was that

while I had above-average capabilities and intelligence, I was an underachiever in school. Or rather, I was an erratic achiever. I did just fine in subjects I liked and couldn't care less about those I didn't. This, of course, frustrated the heck out of my mother and my teachers.

Except for its social aspects, school always seemed like a colossal waste of time. Most of my real learning took place outside of school. I read voraciously, had good friends of all ages and descriptions, was a keen observer and good listener, acquired new skills, wandered as far as my legs and, later on, my bike would carry me, earned money in various creative ways.

As kids, though, we're judged by our school achievements (i.e., grades) rather than those in the greater world. Because I indulged in what **I** wanted to do rather than in what **they** expected of me, they thought I didn't want to do much.

The living of my life has proved them wrong. I have earned academic degrees and professional certifications, and had a number of careers. And I will probably acquire and practice a few more before I quit this planet.

I love learning and becoming proficient at new skills. Then, once I've mastered and practiced them awhile, I want to learn and do something new. I don't necessarily give up on the old things, I just keep adding new ones.

I've been extremely fortunate to have traveled to a great many places in this world, and hope to travel to a lot more.

I seem to need change, newness, variety. And I need

challenges. I've often tackled a thing just to see if I could do it. I need the feeling of accomplishment when I've met the challenge. Of course, that means that I've taken risks and known failure. But that doesn't keep me from continuing to seek out and take on challenges.

People often remark, "Carol, you really are something!" My response is to laugh and say, "Yeah, but nobody's ever been able to figure out what." It's said in jest, but it's true. As soon as they think they've got me pigeonholed, I do a '180' and become something else.

It's also a fact that I usually do several things at once. I'm always juggling at least six projects at a time. And there are always more things on the drawing board.

Not long ago, a friend of mine, a Thai mystic, asked to see my hand. She examined my palm -- a myriad of lines going ever-which-a-way, constantly intersecting and interrupting each other. She nodded and said, "You don't have any choice about all the changes in your life. It's your destiny."

Well, maybe that explains it. Perhaps it's as much a part of my DNA as the color of my eyes or the shape of my toenails. And perhaps it's why I've always been drawn to the new and the different. It's my destiny.

And because of it I've had a wonderful life.

You may find that revealing a life-pattern is useful in discussing your life, as well. Putting a pattern out there at the outset may provide a point of reference for the activities, interests, careers, travels, adventures of your life.

> *Tragedy is something happening to you;*
> *comedy is something happening*
> *to someone else.*
>
> Charlie Chaplin

CELEBRATE THE RIDICULOUS

Sometimes life is ridiculous, and as we have progressed through it, sometimes *we* were ridiculous, too. People may have snickered at us, and now looking back, we can laugh at ourselves as well. Celebrate the ridiculous!

Not only is it healthy to laugh at yourself, but in doing so, you make yourself much more lovable, more interesting, and more real to your readers. You give them a hero to relate to and identify with.

We were all "innocents abroad" at one time. And we've all had "learning experiences" -- incidents which, although perhaps mortifying at the time, we can laugh about now. To paraphrase Charlie Chaplin's great line:

> *Tragedy is something happening to you.*
> *Comedy is tragedy . . . plus time.*

Here's one of my own loss-of-innocence stories. I was 19 years old, on my way to Europe to join my Army-draftee husband in Germany. It was virtually my first foray into the world outside my San Joaquin Valley hometown.

A Hick From the Sticks

New York City's sweltering heat blasted me as I stepped out of Grand Central Station that July day in 1955. Surrounded by my mismatched luggage, I carried everything I couldn't cram into it. On one arm was a heavy wool coat and an oversized purse on one arm. A camera and huge binoculars hung on the opposite shoulder. With my free hand I hailed a taxicab.

A sunflower-yellow cab pulled up and stopped in front of me. The driver just sat behind the wheel, looking at me, like, "Ya want dis cab or not? If ya wannit, then openna damn door and get in!" I opened the back door, struggled to get my heavy suitcases, huge handbag, bulky coat, binoculars and camera into the cab, climbed into the backseat and sat down, closing the door behind me. I told him the name of my hotel and off we drove.

"Where ya from?" he asked. "Yer first trip to New Yawk?" "What're ya here for?"

I answered absently, trying not to appear the proverbial hick craning to gape at the city's skyscrapers.

Once again, in front of the hotel, he just sat, making no move to get out and open my door or offer assistance with my bags, all of which was standard procedure back home.

The meter read $1.55. I handed him two one-dollar bills and held out my hand for change. His jaw dropped. I looked him steadfastly in the eye, moving my hand slightly to indicate that I expected change.

"I gotta eat, lady."

I kept my hand in the same demanding position.

He dropped a nickel into it. "I got kids at home, ya know."

I just stared him in the eye, holding my open hand in his face. Continuing to plead his case, he deposited one nickel at a time until I finally had the full 45 cents. Then I declared, self-righteous as all get-out, "A tip is for **extra** service, not for just doing what you're already getting paid to do!"

I felt downright proud of myself for not letting this city-slicker cab driver take advantage of me. In a bit of a huff, I unloaded all my belongings onto the sidewalk. He drove away, shaking his head.

Two days later, enroute to the S. S. Hollendam for the trans-Atlantic voyage to Rotterdam, I returned to Central Station to pick up the rest of my baggage: a steamer trunk and a footlocker. The ride to the station was the same as before; no assistance from the cabbie.

I asked the driver to wait while I collected my belongings from the baggage dock. A Redcap loaded my luggage onto a cart, which he pushed through the station and out to the sidewalk. He lashed my bulky gear to the rack on the back of the cab. I handed him what I thought was a generous tip -- a couple of bucks.

He held up his hand, like a cop stopping traffic, shook his head, and set me straight. "The standard charge is a buck-fifty per item . . . **plus** a tip.

"Oh!" I flushed hot-flash-fuschia. (I have a feeling we're not in Kansas anymore, Toto.)

I gave him the full amount, plus a bit more, and got back in the cab. All the way through the Holland Tunnel and to the port in New Jersey I sat in shamed silence. When we got to the pier where the Hollendam was moored, I gave this cabbie his full tip, and some extra.

Thus did I learn my first lesson in the ways of the world.

So, there it is, my loss-of-innocence, coming-of-age story. Although I was seriously embarrassed at the time, now I love this story. I love that small-town kid's assertiveness . . . and courage . . . and ability to laugh at herself, even then. Yes, that's me I'm talking about.

That's one of the wonderful things about writing your memoirs. It puts you in touch with yourself -- at all stages of your growth -- as nothing else could, and gives you a better appreciation of yourself.

Tell funny stories on yourself. Celebrate the ridiculous! Invite your reader to laugh at and with you. You'll all feel better for it.

WRITING ABOUT OTHER PEOPLE

Throughout your life you've known a great many people, some of whom may warrant only a mention in passing while others inspire volumes.

Your autobiography is about you, to be sure, but you'll also want to write about the people who influenced you, who inspired you, who had an impact on you -- perhaps a teacher, a preacher, a neighbor, a radio or TV personality or even a stranger who happened to do or say something that changed the way you thought or behaved. You'll want to write about your parents and grandparents, siblings, and maybe other relatives, as well. You'll want to write about your best friend -- and your nemesis; your boss or a co-worker, and others who have crossed your path.

Unless you have lived your life in isolation, your stories about yourself will be about other people too. So lots of people may find their way into your autobiography.

In the pages that follow are some tips on writing about other people. You might find some that will help you make those people, and your stories, more interesting.

YOUR UNIQUE RELATIONSHIPS

Your relationships with the people in your life are truly unique. You know different things about them than anyone else knows. Your adventures with them are one-of-a-kind. They've shared things with you that no one else knows. They've showed you a side of themselves that no one else knows about. As a result, your perception of them is different than anyone else's.

Your experience of your father, for example, was different from that of your siblings. Although you had the same father, your portrayal of him may be someone your siblings barely recognize. There could be many reasons for this:

Your personality is not the same as theirs, so he did not relate to you in the same way as he did to them. He may have punished you differently; he may have discussed philosophy with you but not them; he may have taken your siblings to football games and left you home to shovel snow; he may have adored you and been indifferent to them; the two of you may have been on the same wavelength and laughed at each other's jokes, or had nothing in common at all.

He was at a different stage of life when you came along than when your siblings did, so his daily stresses were not the same. His health may not have been the same. His relationship with your mother may have changed; he may even have had a different wife. His job may have been more (or less) time-consuming and/or stressful. All these things, and much more, affected his personality and temperament. Innumerable variables make your relationship with him unique.

Every human being is so multifaceted that each person who knows a person -- each relative, friend, neighbor, co-worker, etc. -- may know a different person who inhabits that same body.

Even if everyone else has written about a person, your knowledge of and relationship with him or her is like no other's.

So go ahead, write *your* recollections. Tell *your* story.

ANECDOTES TELL THE STORY

When writing about a person, don't just gush or rant about how sweet, charitable, churlish or nasty old "So'n'so" was. *Show it* with an anecdote (a short story or word-picture) that engages your reader and demonstrates just *how* he or she was sweet, charitable, churlish or nasty.

When you write about someone, write scenes, tell tales, paint 'pictures'. Use them to create an image in your readers' minds so that they can fully experience the scene and the person for themselves. An anecdote will tell far more about a person than will just a description or label.

Here's one about my Aunt Bill (Willie Katherine Hartley, 1902 - 1986)

Every year, by the end of May, Aunt Bill's half-acre yard was ablaze with color: gladiolas, zinnias, asters, shasta daisies, larkspur, delphiniums, marguerites, marigolds, stocks, and . . . I don't know what-all.

And roses! Aunt Bill's roses always took prizes at the county fair and Rose Society competitions. People driving by would stop to admire the spectacular array of roses rimming her front yard.

Every year, she'd work all through the night before Memorial Day. She'd have spent the evening picking wheelbarrows-full of the flowers and greenery needed to complete her labor of love and patriotism. To keep them fresh, she'd stand them in galvanized buckets of water. Then, surrounded by their fragrances, she'd go to work in the breezeway making floral arrangements.

Hers were not simple homemade bouquets, nor were they skimpy. Always the artist, Aunt Bill would make dozens of full-blown, elegant arrangements. And as she worked she'd hum or whistle.

Early on Memorial Day, someone would drive her out to the Washington Colony Cemetery where she'd place a bouquet in the sunken metal cylinder on the grave of every veteran. She would see to it that each soldier, sailor and marine buried there was properly honored every Memorial Day.

When she got up in her 80's, arthritis slowed her down. She'd swear in frustration at her stiff fingers as the bouquets painstakingly took shape. And she'd cuss at her creaky knees as she knelt on the graves to place her floral tributes. But she didn't quit until homage was paid to every last veteran lying there.

Instead of an anecdote I could have written a gusher like this: My Aunt Bill was a really good, kind person. You'd have liked her. She was an amazing woman! She was a patriot. She was just fantastic!

All that is true, but does it tell anything about her that you can grab ahold of? Does it give you a picture of her in your mind? Do you get any sense of who she was? If so, you have an amazing imagination; maybe even psychic powers! Most of us need more. We want proof. We want examples that show *how* she was a good person, *why* we would have liked her, *how* she was patriotic, *how* she was fantastic.

On the other side of the coin, here's an anecdote about my stepfather, whom I will call 'LT':

LT loved to goad people until they'd get mad and blow up. Then he'd smirk and boast, "Didn't take me long to get his goat!" I guess it made him feel clever or powerful.

He also thought it was funny to cause pain or trauma. And I was his favorite victim.

Back then, before TV and air conditioning, everyone spent the hot summer evenings outdoors. Huge, hardshelled, hissing, spitting Junebugs buzzed around the porch lights. LT delighted in grabbing a handful of them and stuffing them down my shirt. Then, while I screamed in terror and squirmed in revulsion, he'd throw back his head and laugh, slapping his thigh, enjoying the heck out of my torment.

Now, I could have just said he was a sadistic S.O.B., which is true. (It's just my opinion, of course, but I *am* the author, so I'm entitled.) But there in print is the proof.

This little anecdote shows *how* he was a sadistic S.O.B.

Anecdotes provide the *hows* and the *whys*. They give concrete examples rather than just foggy concepts. 'Sadistic S.O.B.' is nothing but a foggy concept -- a meaningless label. So are 'patriotic', and 'fantastic', and 'good'.

I'm sure you'll agree, it's easier to get a grasp on concrete than it is on fog. It's your anecdotes -- your concrete examples -- that make the people in your stories come alive. They prove your point and make your readers love -- or hate -- the character, right along with you.

Pretend you're in a courtroom: you're the prosecuting attorney. If you merely tell the jury that the defendant is guilty you're going to lose your case. You have to cite evidence, you have to produce exhibits, you have to give data. In other words, you have to prove your case.

So it is in writing. You have to convince the 'judge and jury' (your readers) of the case you're making.

Don't shortchange your readers or your subjects by writing 'fog'. Oh, you can state the concept (the fog, i.e., 'She was patriotic. or He was a jerk.'), but then go ahead and tell the stories that demonstrate the concept. Give them something concrete.

That's how you breathe life into your characters and make them real for your readers.

IN THE BEST OF FAMILIES

So you've got some weird relatives, who doesn't? Nobody's perfect. Everybody's got warts. Some people hide their warts better than others, but everybody's got 'em. Part of what makes people interesting and gives them character is their flaws and inconsistencies, their contradictions, i.e., their 'warts'. So, as you're describing yourself or your other characters, give the full picture. Leave the warts in.

As the old saying goes, "It happens in the best of families."

Surely you want your readers, especially your grandchildren and great-grandchildren, to know the real you, and your other honest-to-goodness real relatives. You don't want them to think you and all their other relatives were saints or angels, do you?

For instance, you may want to write about your ultra-religious grandmother, the straightlaced, proper lady whose public behavior was above reproach, the stern matriarch who viewed anything modern or fun as 'sinful'. Perhaps this same grandma, when she thought no one was looking, nipped at the medicinal brandy, peeked at Uncle Izzy's raunchy magazines, and swore like a tinker when the goat gobbled her sheets on the clothesline.

Now, admit it, isn't that old lady a lot more interesting than when she was just a 'proper lady'?

Your readers, especially your family members, will be delighted to learn about your infamous relatives and friends: the blacksheep, the naughty ones, the outlaws.

And if that blacksheep is you, well, isn't that why you're writing your memoirs in the first place: to tell your side of the story? Maybe you were maligned or misunderstood. Like Gloria Swanson, it's time for you to set the record straight.

The genealogy buffs in my acquaintance are delighted to find a rapscallion in the family tree. The ancestors who just went about their daily life, keeping their noses clean and staying out of trouble, are the norm, of course, in most families. We're happy that most of our ancestors were fine, upstanding people. But if *everyone* in the family was exceptionally virtuous, it could get mighty boring. We need an occasional scalawag in the family bloodline, if only for comic relief.

Of course, one's appreciation for the family's rogues increases with time and distance. If your own parent or sibling is the rascal, your appreciation may be diminished. You may still be embarrassed or humiliated by him or her. You may still harbor anger or resentments toward that person. (If so, write about that, too!)

But by the time future generations are reading about the scamp, the emotional baggage will be gone. They won't be touched by it. They'll probably be relieved to learn that not everyone in the family was perfect. It will take the pressure off them. So if you know some 'scalawag stories' of your ancestors or relatives, go ahead and tell them. Your readers will love it.

I've only recently learned why my mother's family moved from Missouri to California in 1923, when Mom was 15 and her brothers were 17 and 18. As the story goes, one day, the county sheriff came to Grandpa and said, "Bill, if you don't get those boys of yours out of the county by mornin', I'm going to have to arrest 'em."

(It happens in the best of families.)

Grandma and Grandpa, my mom, and her brothers hurriedly packed up and, by dawn the next day, they were on the road to California.

Well, Mom and her siblings are gone now and no one seems to know the rest of the story. My cousins and I have fun conjecturing about it. My guess is that it had something to do with alcohol. It was during Prohibition and I suspect the boys were engaged in bootlegging or moonshining.

My kids and their cousins, and *their* kids, all of whom are generations removed and never knew my uncles, are tickled pink to hear about them. They add a tasty bit of spice to the family "soup."

Of course, you may not want to open the closet door too wide and reveal *all* the family's skeletons, especially

113

if someone you care about would be hurt by it. If, for instance, Uncle Bud was a real louse, but Mom loved her brother Bud and forgave him anything, you may decide to soft-pedal a bit on the subject of Uncle Bud.

If, on the other hand, Mom is no longer with us, or if Uncle Bud's 'louseness' is an important element of your story, you may decide to go ahead and tell it. Or you may write about it now but not show that part to Mom. Or you may write about it and sit down with Mom, read it to her and have a long-overdue talk. (That's my recommendation.)

Only you can decide how much you are willing to censor yourself, if at all. You may simply decide to tell all and let the chips fall where they may.

*History will be kind to me
for I intend to write it.*
Winston Churchill

QUIRKS & IDIOSYNCRACIES

Along with their flaws and inconsistencies, please write about your characters' quirks and idiosyncracies. You may not even be aware of your own eccentric traits and mannerisms, so you probably won't write about them. But you are aware of other people's. Include them in your stories. It will make the characters much more real to your readers, and much more fun.

In recent movies, one of the more memorable characters is Sally (Meg Ryan) in *When Harry Met Sally*. When ordering in a restaurant she was always very specific, and requested some things to be served "on the side". While that may not be the thing you remember ***most*** about 'Sally', I'm sure you'll agree that her little idiosyncracy in restaurant ordering *helped* make her memorable.

In *As Good As It Gets*, Melvin (Jack Nicholson) was a neurotic who would avoid stepping on a crack in the sidewalk, and who used a brand new bar of soap every time he washed his hands. Quirky, but interesting.

My little anecdote about my Aunt Bill states, ". . . as she worked she'd hum or whistle."

These touches humanize a character and make him or her more vivid in your readers' minds and experience.

Writing Activity:

Write about a person.

◆ Pick the person who will be your topic.
◆ Use 'The Balloon Method' to remember everything you can about him/her.
◆ Decide what you want your reader to know about that person.
◆ Let your reader know what your relationship with him/her was.
◆ Write an anecdote (or several), paint word-pictures, with concrete examples to make your case.
◆ Write about how that person influenced, inspired, impacted you and your life: what he/she meant to you.
◆ Tell what was unique or unusual about him or her.
◆ Humanize him/her with flaws, inconsistencies, contradictions, quirks, idiosyncracies. Leave the 'warts' in.
◆ Use dialogue. Put words in his/her mouth. It will give him/her both character and personality.
◆ Have fun!

THE HARDEST PART OF WRITING

At times, as you know, life is ***not*** just a bowl of cherries; sometimes it's the pits! And you will be doing yourself and your readers a great disservice if you only include the sweet parts and discard the pits.

If not for the tough times and/or the people who maligned or mistreated you, you would not be the person you are today. Adversity can strengthen a person. It is often through adversity that one gains wisdom. It's been said that "Adversity is God's university". Sharing your misfortune with your readers is an opportunity to pass along your hard-won wisdom.

Every film or novel worth its salt has an antagonist -- a villain or treacherous situation or condition. Set the stage, introduce the antagonist, show the steps leading to your loss, misfortune, mistreatment, humiliation, tragedy, ruination, betrayal, shock, injustice. Demonstrate how you dealt with it and were transformed by it. That's the drama in your story.

Note the events that were catalysts for change, and your reactions, feelings and conflicts which demonstrate the growth that came about as a result of those events.

By telling about your tough times you may become vulnerable, but that's not a bad thing. If readers are going to care about you and your life, you must allow them to become emotionally involved. It's largely the telling of the difficulties in your life and how you dealt with them, that accomplishes that. Without emotion in your writing, you're just a reporter -- a detached observer.

Frank McCourt, author of the moving work, *Angela's Ashes*, says, "Telling the truth is the hardest part of writing." But that didn't keep him from doing it. *Angela's Ashes* tells of his painfully impoverished childhood, his drunken, abusive father, his disgraced, humiliated mother, and his brothers, all suffering through. He wrote about how he coped with all this and how he felt about it.

Angela's Ashes won the Pulitzer Prize for Literature, was on the New York Times Bestsellers List for a very long time, and was made into a movie.

Who knows, maybe someday we'll be seeing your story on bestsellers lists or in a movie. It may even win a Pulitzer Prize. It could happen!

Sometimes life is the pits!

I WANT YOU TO LEAVE

Sue Denim, Tucson, Arizona

I don't want to be married anymore.
>Yeah, that's right. I don't.
>I want you to leave. Now. Go!

You look stunned. You're hurt. You're angry.
>You're feeling rejected and unloved.
>You're confused.

Well, turnabout's fair play, for
>right after the "I do's"
>you started with the "I don't's."

"I don't love you."
>>"I don't want to make love to you."
>>"I don't care about *your* needs."

I was stunned. *I* was hurt. *I* was angry.
>*I* felt rejected and unloved.
>And, boy, was I confused!

Why did you marry me
>and bind my life to yours,
>only to use me and abuse me?

I thought, *If only I can be perfect*
>*-- sweet and sexy and fun --*
>*then surely he will love me.*

So I jumped through hoops to please you,
>knocked myself out day-by-day.
>You ***never*** tried to please me.

No, you ravaged me with rage,
>rejection and rebuke, you
>raped my soul with bogus love.

Since day-one I've been your yo-yo.
    You distance me, discard me.
    When you need me you retrieve me.

Since day-one I've felt so hurt,
    so rejected, so unloved,
    so damned confused!

Hmmm.... *Now* you say you *love* me,
    you cannot *live* without me.
    That's not love! That's selfish fear.

Love is connection and caring
    support, growth and sharing.
    I doubt you know how to love.

You do know how to destroy,
    to disparage, diminish, disdain.
    My heart is dead ... and with it, love.

So I don't want to be married anymore.
    Yeah, that's right. I don't.
    I want you to leave. Now. Go.

Now I'm not angry or hurt or confused.
    I'm just weary. Done in. Burnt out.
    Now it's time to take care of *me*.

I'm going to need to rebuild myself,
    To revive the parts that died.
    I must relearn to love myself.

So I don't want to be married anymore.
    Yeah, that's right. I don't.
    I just want you to leave ... now.

YOUR YELLOW-BRICK ROAD

How did you become the person you are today? As you've gone through life, internal changes have occurred; changes in your world-view, changes in your character and attitude. That's what your readers *really* want to know about. They want to follow your growth to gain insight into the person you have become.

They want to know about the incidents and situations that brought about the changes in your character, and maybe even changed the course of your life. But keep in mind, it was not the events that changed you. It was your thoughts and emotions regarding them, and your subsequent decisions and actions. The incident itself was neutral. It's how you *felt* about and *responded* to it that's the story!

The situation or event is merely the hatrack on which to hang your story. The story is YOU!

The classic movie, *The Wizard of Oz* is a great metaphor for life and an excellent model for an autobiography, a short story or anecdote, or all of the above.

As you're constructing your story, let the reader in on:
- your <u>*goal or objective*</u> -- which may change as you go along, as Dorothy's did, but be sure the reader knows

what it is.

- the *start of your journey* -- your conflict or trouble-some situation, your decision and subsequent actions.
- the *turning points, roadblocks, obstacles, detours, landmarks and signposts*.
- your *perils and conflicts* on the way to accomplishing your goal.
- the *people or elements* who/which assisted you.
- your *arrival at your destination* (the goal -- your Emerald City).
- your *thoughts, emotions and inner conflicts* through the course of your journey.
- your *inner changes*: how you grew in wisdom, courage, strength, confidence, compassion, maturity, *et cetera*.
- how your *goal was accomplished.*

Let your reader know how you traveled your own "yellow-brick road" to reach your own "Emerald City." (This is discussed further in the section titled, 'Elements of a Good Story'.)

This can be done in a simple anecdote or a whole book or screenplay. The following short story by James Walters of Minden, NV, is a small example:

My Fingers Know Where to Go

A few years ago, I attended a concert by Danish pianist and humorist Victor Borge. That night on stage, he said that people often asked him how, at nearly 90, he could still play so well. He told them, "I don't even have to think about it. My fingers know where to go."

By the time I left the concert hall his statement was forgotten. I wasn't aware that my subconscious mind had filed it away for future use.

Some time later, a year-or-so ago, as a way of processing grief, I decided to learn to play the piano. I had taken lessons as a child but had resisted mightily. I'd simply refused to practice. Playing the same piece over and over was boring; tedious. I'd rather be out playing ball or riding my bike. I'd escape as soon as I could. So, as an adult, of course, I couldn't play the piano or even read music. I tried to learn a few times but always gave up.

Now 64, I started again, this time, determined to learn. I knew where 'Middle-C' was on the piano and on a sheet of music, and was forced to locate every other note relative to it. Laboriously, note-by-note, I set about learning to play Beethoven's *Für Elise*. (I was unwilling to spend time on a piece I didn't want to listen to.) And I practiced.

When I'd tire of practicing and ache to stop, Mr. Borge's voice would rise up out of my subconscious. I would hear him say, "My fingers know where to go," and I would wonder, how many **hundreds** of times did he have to play a piece before his fingers knew where to go? His message was this: repetition is the key to success. So I'd do repetitions until **my** fingers knew where to go.

I'd play it once more. And then I'd play it again.

A long time after that concert, Victor Borge changed my way of thinking about playing the piano, which in turn, changed my practicing habits. He provided the motivation I needed in order to persevere. Without his words inside my head I surely would have given up.

I still hear them when I get bored or frustrated with a piece of music. And I still ask myself, how many hundreds of times did he have to play a piece for his fingers to know where to go?

And I play it once more. And I play it again.

I'll never be a Paderewski or a Victor Borge, but I can play the piano well enough for my own enjoyment. And it got me through my grieving.

Let's examine this little anecdote in terms of the Yellow-Brick Road model on the previous page:

◆ *Goals/Objectives:* The author's desire to **process grief** and to **learn to play the piano** provided his goals.

◆ *Start of Journey:* His **decision** to learn to play the piano got him started.

◆ *Roadblocks/Obstacles:* His **boredom, frustration**; his **history of quitting** could have defeated him.

◆ *Helper/Inspirer/Motivator:* His **subconscious mind; Victor Borge** helped keep him going.

◆ *Peril/Conflict:* His **desire to quit practicing** conflicted with his **desire to play** the piano.

◆ *Thoughts/Emotions:* His **realization** that practice is the key. His **determination** to do repetitions until his fingers knew where to go kept him practicing.

◆ *Arrival at destination:* He can **play the piano**. His

grieving is past. He is **satisfied** and feels the **pride of accomplishment**.

- *Growth/Change/Transformation:* His **level of determination increased** as did his **willingness to persevere**. His **musical ability improved**.

To repeat myself, the event itself was neutral. It was neither grief nor Mr. Borge's statement that produced the change. Everyone at that concert heard the same words, and surely there were others there who were grieving, but I doubt that all were similarly affected. It was the personalizing of it, the *Aha!* -- the decision, and the subsequent actions that brought about the author's change and growth.

In bringing your readers along with you on your own yellow-brick road -- your path to who you've become -- you're giving your readers what they *really* want, which is the chance to know you.

> *Your life is determined*
> *not so much by*
> *what happens to you*
> *as it is by*
> *how you respond to*
> *what happens to you.*

An historical event

KENNEDY'S BEEN SHOT

Walter Cronkite, TV Newsman, New York, NY

. . . the first bulletin came over the UPI wire from Dallas: "Three shots were fired at President Kennedy's motorcade in downtown Dallas."

Almost immediately another UPI lead said it appeared that President Kennedy had been "seriously wounded . . . perhaps fatally wounded" in the shooting and that the motorcade had broken from its intended route and seemed to be on the way to a hospital.

Ed shouted the flashes to me and I shouted to the whole newsroom. "Kennedy's been shot. Let's get on the air!" But it turned out we couldn't get on the air immediately. . . . I headed for a radio booth in the next room, and from there broadcast the first television announcement of the assassination attempt.

. . . For the first hour, a shocked nation hung on the sketchy details from the hospital as it became clear that the President was in critical condition. And then came the Barker-Rather report from outside the emergency room that they had learned the President was dead. We were still debating in New York whether we should put such a portentous but unofficial announcement on the air when, within minutes, the hospital issued a bulletin confirming the news. It fell to me to make the announcement.

It is an interesting thing about us newspeople. We are much like doctors and nurses and firemen and police. In the midst of tragedy our professional drive takes over and dominates our emotions. We move almost like automatons to get the job done. The time for an emotional reaction must wait.

I was doing fine in that department until it was necessary to pronounce the words, "From Dallas, Texas, the flash -- apparently official: President Kennedy died at 1 p.m., Central Standard Time -- a half-hour ago (pause) . . .

The words stuck in my throat. A sob wanted to replace them. A gulp or two quashed the sob, which metamorphosed into tears forming in the corner of my eyes. I fought back the emotion and regained my professionalism, but it was touch and go there for a few seconds before I could continue. "Vice President Johnson has left the hospital in Dallas . . . . Presumably, he will be taking the oath of office shortly and become the thirty-sixth President of the United States."

I was on the air for six hours when our producer, Don Hewitt, said Charles Collingwood was there to relieve me briefly. As I got up from my chair, I realized for the first time that I was still in my shirtsleeves, my tie loosened at the collar, far more informal than I would normally appear on the air. My secretary had slipped my jacket onto the back of my chair but I had not noticed, and so intense were those hours that no one else even mentioned my dishabille.

I went into my glass-walled office off the newsroom intending to call Betsy. I needed an intimate moment to share emotions. Millions of Americans were doing the same thing. All afternoon I had been reporting that telephone lines were jammed and switchboards clogged across the nation. I had not thought this would create a problem for me . . .

A Reporter's Life. Alfred A. Knopf, New York NY. 1996.

The man who writes about himself and his own time is the only man who writes about all men and about all time.

George Bernard Shaw

ALWAYS LEAVE 'EM WANTIN' MORE

Just because something happened doesn't mean you have to write about it. Be selective. Make sure you're telling a story, not merely making a report.

> *Drama is life with all the dull bits cut out.*
> Alfred Hitchcock

A good memoir is drama, so throw out your dull bits.

You'll probably want to do some serious editing before you go to print. As you read through what you've written, ask yourself, am I telling too much? Is what I've written going to hold my reader's interest?

A lot of writers, especially novices, fall in love with their own words. When they get something down on paper it's as if it's the Rosetta Stone. It has become sacrosanct by the very act of writing it. They can't bear to let any of it go.

While it's true that you want to set the stage for the scene and paint a picture with your words, and you want to include information that will allow your readers to experience it fully, you don't want to bury them in 'dull bits'. That's the surest way to lose them.

As they used to say in vaudeville, "Always leave 'em wantin' more."

> *The secret of being tiresome is in telling everything.*
> Voltaire

TRUTH IS IN THE EYE OF THE BEHOLDER

I once knew a fourth-grade teacher who arranged for an accomplice to open the door in the middle of class and release a cage full of pigeons into the classroom. You can imagine the chaos that ensued as the kids tried to catch or dodge the birds!

The purpose of this rather bizarre episode was to set up a writing exercise. When everything had calmed down and the birds were removed, the children wrote about their experience. The event was not discussed. The kids just took pen in hand and wrote about it.

As you might imagine, each story was different from every other one. And each story was absolutely true. While it was a shared experience, it belonged uniquely to each child.

We all have our own truth. We all see things from our own point of view.

Whatever you write, there may be someone else who will say, "That's not how it happened! Here's how it really was . . . " But that's *their* truth.

You're writing *your* story: what you remember, your perceptions, what you know.

You are writing from *your* experience. You are writing *your* recollections about a person, place or thing, or an incident, situation or era. If others disagree with you, let them write their own story!

ACCESSORIZE

In addition to writing what you remember you may want to 'accessorize' a bit in order to paint a picture, set the scene, create the mood and invite your reader in.

It's like a woman dressing for a special event. She puts on her 'little black dress'. It's okay, but not stunning. Then she begins to accessorize. She slips on ultra-sheer black hose and high-fashion shoes, adds jewelry or a scarf, and completes the ensemble with a *chic* hat, gloves and bag.

The basic dress and shoes are the bare essentials. It's by adding the accessories, however, that she is increasing her chances of being noticed and fully appreciated.

It's the same with your story. The story's 'basic dress and shoes' are the bare facts. As a writer you can enhance it by dressing it up. You can allow your imagination to drift a bit in order to create the accessories.

When I wrote the anecdote below, there was a lot I didn't remember. When writing this story I merely embellished my actual recollections with some *'what-could-have-beens':*

The Only Stereo System We Knew

When I was a kid, the only stereo system we knew about was not something you listened to, it was something you looked through. It was a wondrous contraption and it was all the entertainment my sister and I could have hoped for on a sizzling summer afternoon.

The coolest place in our central valley farmhouse was my grandmother's bedroom on the north side of the house, shaded by big old umbrella trees. If there was any breeze at all, it came through the open windows, fluttering the lace curtains and riffling the roses in the pitcher on the washstand. Beneath her step-up walnut bed was a wooden box which she brought out infrequently. If it had been an everyday event, it would have taken away from it. No, it was special and, to us, quite magical.

One scorching day the summer 'Patsy' turned 7 and I was almost 5, Grandma invited us into her room where the scents of fresh roses, lavender sachet and Old English greeted us. She had a surprise. With smiling eyes, my tiny Danish grandmother, herself smelling of Rosewater & Glycerin, knelt beside the bed, her joints stiff and her movements awkward. Carefully lifting the crocheted bedspread, she pulled the box out from underneath. She lifted the lid and exposed its contents as if revealing Aladdin's treasure. Excitement tickled through our small bodies.

In the box was a strange apparatus, a stereopticon, and, with it, a stack of postcard-sized photographs. The stereopticon consisted of a metal eyepiece similar in shape to a snorkeling mask; underneath it was a wooden handle and, extending out front, a wooden slider. Atop that was the picture holder, which could be positioned for focus.

The photographs were unique, as well. They were sepia-toned side-by-side twin-photos, some of which were hand-painted in vibrant colors. There were photos of the boardwalk at Atlantic City, Native Americans in their tribal village, Hawaiian Islanders in grass skirts, Victorian-era men and women in a 'horseless carriage'. And there were nature scenes: Niagra Falls, Rocky Mountain bighorn sheep, Yosemite's Half Dome.

The amazing thing about the stereopticon and its stereo-images was that when you put the pictures in and gazed through it, they sprang to life! They became three-dimensional! They were so real you could virtually walk into the scene. I still don't understand how those flat photos came to life like that. All I know is that they did.

That day, after opening the box and removing its contents, Grandma actually left the room, trusting us to enjoy its wonders unattended, making us feel very grown-up and quite special. We sat on the hardwood floor of Grandma's bedroom, our bare legs grateful for its smooth coolness, and spent the afternoon engrossed in the enthralling images. The heat was forgotten. We were cooled by Niagra Falls' mist, by the wind as we raced along in the horseless carriage, by the ocean breeze in Atlantic City.

To be perfectly honest, I don't remember what kind of curtains were on the window. I have no idea what kind of wood constituted my grandmother's bed, or if it was the step-up kind. I don't know if there were roses on the washstand or if the box under the bed was wood. There are plenty of things I don't remember, so I just let my imagination wander. I asked myself, W*hat could have been?*

I wanted to create a scene my readers could enter into and experience along with me. So I included some visual and sensory details to help them along. I wanted them to see it, feel it, smell it, hear it. Not only did accessorizing not detract from the story, I think it enriched it.

Was I lying by including details that may not have been strictly true? No, of course not. I was merely dressing up the facts to make my story more appealing to my readers.

My *what-could-have-beens* were consistent with what I did remember and with *what-probably-was,* so it worked. We lived in a Victorian farmhouse, filled with lovely yet simple things. If we had lived in a tar-paper shack or a palatial mansion my *what-could-have-beens* might be inconsistent and therefore not believable.

Literary license or *creative non-fiction* allows a writer to take some liberties with the facts in order to improve upon the story and enhance their readers' enjoyment. It's still the truth. It's still what really happened. In no way was the integrity of the story compromised. It is just told in a way that is more experiential and more enjoyable.

When that story ran in **55-plus!**, a senior magazine in the San Francisco Bay Area, several readers wrote in to say they felt as if they were right there in that room with those two little girls. So, you see, it worked!

<u>A word of caution</u>: If there is something in your story that is inconsistent -- a *'what couldn't (or shouldn't) have been'*, be sure to comment on it. If you mention the crystal chandelier in Grandpa's log cabin, be sure to explain its presence. (That's a story in itself!) If you neglect to, your reader will be jarred by it and may even question your sanity.

Writing Activity:

Write on any topic you wish, employing the arts of 'seduction' and 'accessorizing'. (And any other 'Spice Up Your Life' techniques you can.)

◆ **Seduction**: Lead your reader on. Drop hints about things to come. Make the reader so curious about what's going to happen they'll be flippin' those pages like mad.

◆ **Accessorizing**: Embelish your story. Dress it up a little to give your reader a real feel for it. Describe the setting -- paint word pictures -- using sensory devices. Make your reader smell, taste, hear, feel and see whatever is going on in the story.

◆ **Thoughts & Feelings**: Let your reader know what you (or your other characters) were thinking and feeling about whatever is going on in your story. Make your reader feel something for the character(s).

◆ Have fun!

ELEMENTS OF A GOOD STORY

What makes a story good? What elements do your favorite books, movies and plays have in common?

For starters, let's look at the basics of any story:
- it has a beginning, a middle, and an end.
- it is self-contained.
- it has a point.

But beyond those most elementary basics of a story -- good, bad or indifferent -- let's look at the elements of a *good* story:

- **Introduction**: sets the stage; establishes the time and place for the action; invites the reader or viewer in.
- **Hook**: the ploy used to grab the readers' or audience's attention and get them hooked. Then the writer just reels them into the main part of the story.
- **Action**: what happens; what the characters do, say or think. Action is what keeps the readers' interest.
- **Goal or Mission**: the hero's dream or purpose, somthing he or she is working toward, a feat to be accomplished. It gives meaning and purpose to the story and moves the action forward. It provides the plot.
- **Protagonist**: the hero (male or female); the good guy; the sympathetic character. In your autobiography the protagonist is, of course, you. You're the one the reader relates to, sympathizes with and roots for.
- **Co-protagonist**: the hero's ally and associate, who assists, supports and accompanies the hero in accomplishing the all-important goal or mission.

sists, supports and accompanies the hero in accomplishing the all-important goal or mission.

- **Antagonist(s)**: the bad-guy, the anti-hero, the villain. The antagonist is that which threatens the hero or obstructs the hero's mission. It can be a person or group of people, or it can be a situation, e.g., a storm, poverty, sickness, disability, addiction, societal scorn, *et cetera.*
- **Tension/Conflict/Struggle/Suspense**: that which keeps readers or viewers on the edge of their seats and keeps them turning pages.
- **Humor**: comic relief. Laughter is an important element in a story, especially to relieve built-up tension.
- **Thoughts/Emotions**: readers learn who the hero really is and how he/she is changing through his/her thoughts and feelings.
- ★**Transformation**: inner changes in the hero during the course of the story. <u>This is the most important element in any story</u>. The growth may be in terms of courage, inner-strength, maturity, wisdom, trustworthiness, confidence, determination, kindness, sophistication, inner-peace, self-esteem, *et cetera.*
- **Conclusion/Resolution**: the drama is resolved and the story comes to an end.

To demonstrate these elements, let's look briefly at The Wizard Of Oz:

- In the **Introduction** we get acquainted with the hero: Dorothy, her family and friends, and the setting: rural on the head, ends up in a land of fantasy and jeopardy when things go from the familiar to the astonishing.

- The **Action** is constant. Dorothy runs away from home, then returns, lands in OZ and spends the rest of the story in and out of peril, trying to reach the Emerald City, then completing preposterous tasks and overcoming impossible obstacles in order to get back home to Kansas. There's plenty of action.

- Dorothy's **Goal** or **Mission**, at the beginning, is to save her dog Toto from the clutches of Miss Gulch. Once she lands in OZ, however, her overriding goal is to return to the peace and comfort of her home and family in Kansas. Her companions also have goals: a heart, a brain, courage.

- Our **Protagonist** is Dorothy.

- The **Co-Protagonists** are The Good Witch Glynda, The Scarecrow, The Tin Woodman, The Cowardly Lion and The Wizard of OZ.

- The **Antagonist,** in the beginning, is Miss Gulch. Then, once Dorothy is in the Land of OZ, the Wicked Witch of the West takes over that all-important role.

- **Tension/Conflict/Struggle/Suspense** are provided throughout as Dorothy and her companions get into one perilous situation after another and we wonder how (or if) they're going to escape or overcome it. The witch's wickedness, along with the bizarre happenings in this very peculiar land conspire to keep Dorothy and her companions from achieving their goals.

- Throughout the story, **Humor** is provided by the antics of the Wizard, Scarecrow, Tin Woodman, Lion, and a very cleverly written script.
- We gain insight into Dorothy's **Thoughts and Feelings** as she agonizes over her plight, expresses astonishment at the odd goings-on in the curious land, voices terror and doubt as she is tested, declares faith in her companions and the Wizard, and longs for her Kansas home.
- ★Dorothy's **Transformation** comes about through her realization that there's no place like home, and that she has always possessed the power to return.
- The **Conclusion or Resolution** occurs when, after multiple hazards and terrors, Dorothy and her companions complete the tasks set by the Wizard, and the wicked witch is dead. The Wizard himself is debunked, her companions realize that they already have what they longed for, and Dorothy and Toto are back home in Kansas.

Although <u>all</u> of these elements may not be present in <u>every</u> good story, <u>*nearly* all</u> of them are found in all good stories.

As you're writing your stories, you might refer back to these pages from time to time and make use of the above elements of a good story. Or, having written a story, you might want to check to see how many of them you've instinctively used. I think you'll be amazed to find that they're already there.

You've always had within you the power, and the ability, to tell a really good story.

To be sure, writing autobiographically may be different from writing a novel or screenplay, so some of this may not apply to *everything* you write. Autobiographical writings may at times be a series of recollections, or an introspective retrospective, an essay, or any number of other things rather than merely a story.

However, when you do write a story, keep these elements in mind. To be a 'good read', your memoir needs to be a good story or a series of good stories, as well as whatever else you choose to include.

Writing Activity:

Write a story using an event as the "hatrack". Use as many of the 12 Elements in the previous section as you can. Pay special attention to "Transformation". The story can be any length. The event can be an incident that made the front page of the newspaper or one that is known only to you.

◆ Use "The Balloon Method" to help you remember everything you can about the event.

◆ Show your character's (your) motivation, goal, dream, and how he/she/you accomplished it.

◆ Build in some tension, conflict, suspense.

◆ Transformation: Show how you and others changed over the course of the story: what you learned; how you grew.
(As you have read through the little stories in this book, you have seen many examples showing how the characters became smarter, wiser, braver, more persevering, more serene, more confident, *et cetera*.)

◆ Have fun!

Stories my mother told me

PLEASE DON'T KILL MY DADDY!

Ronald V. Allen, Reno, NV

Scariff is a small village on the River Shannon in Ireland. In 1917, *The Black & Tans* -- British soldiers so-named for the color of the uniforms -- were the occupation troops.

On a warm night in June of that year while the curfew was in force, a donkey was braying in the night. Michael Gleeson went out the back door of his cottage at Number 7 Bridge Street. He slipped along the pathway behind the row houses and found the donkey. As quietly as he could, he took the now-calm beast to a stable where there was food, water and shelter.

He was spotted by the British soldiers, though, and had to make a run for it.

Margaret, his daughter, who was 7 years old, was terrified that he would be caught . . . . or worse, shot by the soldiers. As he came in through the kitchen and then up the stairs to the bedroom, she thought of the rifle buried in the backyard. She could hear her mother scolding Michael for doing such a dangerous thing and was glad it was over.

Then, a shout from the street. "Come out, Gleeson! We know it was you!"

Silence.

Then, finally, "If it's me you want, Rigby, come and get me!" roared the voice from upstairs.

"Oh God! No!" screamed little Margaret, sensing how bad the situation was.

Captain Rigby spurred his horse toward the front door and stopped with the horse's hooves on the front step, and the horse and Rigby looking into the front room.

"Surround the place," he ordered. His men started to go.

Margaret was at the front door, right by the huge horse.

"Come out, Gleeson."

"Never."

"Please don't kill my daddy!" pleaded little Margaret.

At that moment, Rigby's eyes and Margaret's met and in that fleeting instant, compassion and reason overtook conflict and rules.

"Hold it, men," commanded Rigby. The tall young British officer leaned down to the little girl, and with a lump in his throat he said, "Don't cry, little one. I've a little girl just like you, and I'm not going to hurt your daddy."

He backed the horse off the step and onto the cobblestone street. As the horse turned, Captain Rigby looked back and, as if to acknowledge her courage, tipped his riding crop to his cap and rode away.

Margaret Gleeson, that little girl, was my mother.

BLUEPRINT FOR A GREAT NOVEL OR PLAY

> *There are three rules for writing the novel.*
> *Unfortunately, no one knows what they are.*
>
> W. Somerset Maughm

It would be presumptuous for me or anyone else to say, "I have the formula for a great book or film." For whatever rule or formula one devises, there are many exceptions. However, there is a formula that has worked well for many a successful novel or play.

Perhaps most of us will write only an autobiography -- a Birth-to-Present-Day chronicle, or vignettes of the bits and pieces of our lives, such as those in this book. For those who are a bit more ambitious, however, and wish to write a novel or play about a piece of their lives, the structure on the next page may be helpful.

Fitting your story into this structure improves it. It makes it far more exciting and turns it into a page-turner. It's simple (though it may not be easy!). Try it. You may end up with a bestseller, mega-movie or Broadway play. (It works well for the short story, too.)

Before you start writing, give your story some thought. Picture it in terms of this structure -- along with the 'Elements of a Good Story', of course. (They're compatible.) Map it out with this structure in mind.

Screenwriter William Goldman said, "Screenplays are structure." Period. So are novels and stageplays.

The structure looks like this:

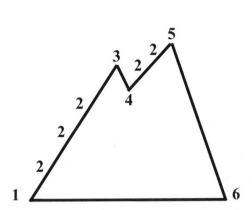

1. **The inciting moment**. The situation or action that gets the story going and gets the reader or audience involved. (The hook.)
2. **Complications.** Pile 'em on. Get your hero in a lot of trouble, then pile on some more.
3. **Crisis**. The situation is terrible. Tension is high.
4. **Reversal**. Back off a little, relieve the tension a bit, then spike it.
5. *Catastrophe!* Gadzooks, things can't get any worse!
6. **Solution & conclusion.** The problem is solved and everybody's happy (except the villain). *The End*. Roll the credits.

From now on, as you read a novel or watch a play on stage, screen or TV, be aware of these 6 'building blocks'. See how often this structure is used to create a truly gripping story.

The French playwright, 'Scribe', used the following as his 'structure':

- ◆ Get your character up in a tree with alligators underneath;
- ◆ Throw rocks at him;
- ◆ Get him out of the tree.

As you see, it's the same idea as the 'blueprint' on the previous page. But what does this have to do with writing autobiographically?

It is said that all books are autobiographical. Every writer draws on his or her own experience and conclusions. What else <u>could</u> one draw upon?

Creativity is real life expanded by one's imagination. It starts with what we know -- what we have experienced and observed -- and extends outward from there. It can extend as far in any direction as you, the writer, care to take it. It can be as benign or as bizarre as you wish; as sentimental or terrifying; as tame or thrilling.

Even writers like Stephen King, whose creativity and imagination seem to know no bounds, start with real life. If they didn't, readers couldn't relate to their stories and characters, and their books wouldn't get read.

Use your own real-life stories as your starting point and expand upon them. Use your imagination.

The 'blueprint' on the preceding page works well for any *genre:* mystery, drama, comedy, adventure, horror, romance, science fiction, fantasy. And don't forget children's books.

Try superimposing it upon one of your own life dramas. I think the result will surprise and delight you.

Writing Activity:

Write a story using the structure on the previous pages. Any topic.

- Pick a topic: a situation or event out of your past.
- Use The Balloon Method to help your recall.
- Start off with a bang. Get right into the story with 'the inciting moment'. Lay out your hero's problem early-on. (In the first sentence, if possible.) Get hero taking action toward solving it right way.
- Demonstrate that your hero *really* wants to solve the problem; tell why s/he *must* solve it; what will happen if s/he doesn't. Make the stakes high.
- Introduce the other important characters. Give them and your hero quirks, idiosyncracies.
- Make your antagonist as nasty/terrible as you can. Remember, the antagonist can be a person, or poverty, bigotry, illness, the weather, etc., or an animal . . . (or an 'alien'?).
- Build the tension. Pile on the complications.
- Accessorize. Enhance your story -- embellish facts, as necessary. Bring in sensory details.
- Engage the reader's emotions; reveal hero's thoughts & feelings.
- Seduce your reader. Hint about what's to come.
- Make your reader wonder if your hero can/will "get out of that tree". Throw 'rocks' at him/her **&** the snapping alligators! Use cliffhangers.
- Solve the problem. Get your hero "out of the tree."
- Have fun!

THE ULTIMATE CONCLUSION

Of course, in real life, things don't always get wrapped up in a neat little package with all the loose ends tied up as they do in most novels or films. Sometimes in real life the villain wins or one's goal is not accomplished. Nevertheless, there are conclusions. And you can write about them.

There may have been times in your life when you didn't win, when someone or something did you in and you were forced to move on. As you're well aware, the end of one episode is the beginning of another. In your autobiography, you can show how you dealt with your disappointments or crises. You can demonstrate how you turned things around and prevailed despite "failure." You can describe how you kept on going, or pivoted and went in a different direction.

You can write about how a tragedy or failure was a blessing in disguise: how it opened the door to a new path and how you adapted and grew because of it, or how you coped with it, and how it helped shape the person you are today.

If you are still around to read this, the ultimate conclusion, of course, hasn't happened yet. As I tell my kids, "It ain't over 'til it's over!" All kinds of wonderful things can still happen and, I firmly believe, will.

There's bound to be at least one more chapter or story, maybe even a novel or screenplay in your life. What it will be is up to you.

NOTE IDEAS ASAP

I recommend that you get in the habit of carrying a hand-held tape recorder or small notebook and pen with you at all times. You never know when a memory will surface; when an aroma will waft across your path, a song will play on the car radio, or your mind will be wandering and a memory will emerge, or someone will say something that makes you think of something from your past. *Viola!* There's a piece of your life story.

I find that while driving long distances or zipping along a familiar route, my mind wanders, and sometimes something wonderful will pop into it. If I wait until I get where I'm going, though, it's evaporated, vanished into thin air. No matter how hard I wrack my brain trying to recapture whatever it was, it's forgotten, never to return.

A small tape recorder comes in very handy. I keep it on the seat beside me so that when a thought occurs I can grab the tape recorder, press the ***Record*** button and talk for a few seconds. Then, when I get home, my idea is right there with me. I haven't had to risk an accident to get the thought noted.

Take it to bed with you, too. Some of our best ideas come in the middle of the night.

I don't recommend the voice-activated feature on some recorders. By the time it hears your voice, figures out that you have something to say and gets itself up-and-running, you've said the memory-jogger word or phrase, and your recorder has missed it.

Grief, Pets

The Leash That Meant GO!

Jeann McDuffie, Santa Rosa, CA

The soft brown eyes looked up, expecting my help in dealing with the foreboding force within his body.

I can do nothing but stroke that great noble head as I've done countless times before . . . searching out the special spot behind his ear where the hair is puppy-soft, like goosedown.

The ominous gurgling sound of his breathing. The shudders than run unchecked through his once-powerful body. And the eyes, those soft brown eyes still expecting my help. Expecting me to know without words just what he wants and needs. But this time, old friend, I cannot help.

I get his collar and leash, and his tail goes **Whump** against the floor. The leash means **GO!**

Then the blood. From deep inside, it gushes from his mouth in violent spurts, forming bubbly red splotches on the gray porch.

Brilliant. Incongruously beautiful. Deadly.

Our Rebel is dying.

Pure instinct gets him to the car, but his legs fail. I lift him inside; hoping there's still a chance. Knowing there's not. Oh, please!

Life leaves him in a few soft jerks of that beloved body, and final release in the soft brown eyes that, to the end, look to me for help. Not accusing, not doubting. just trusting.

Now it is I who ask for help. Help to ease the heart-ache of feeling this familiar tawny body so slack and life-less against my legs.

Reb, how we'll miss you.

Back home to clean the porch. To wash and scrub and wash some more, letting the rush of water take away the crimson splashes of blood that were life -- and death -- for our Reb.

How to tell the others? I cringe at the thought of passing to the ones I love this heavy sadness.

And so, the final act of acceptance. I put away the food dish, the water dish, the blanket and the bed . . . and the leash that meant *GO!*

GET AN EDITOR

Every writer needs an editor. Let me repeat that. **Every writer needs an editor.**

Professional writers would not think of going to press without one, and novices shouldn't either. Two or more heads are better than one. It's always a good idea to have someone else read your work and make corrections and suggestions. Fellow writers are best. They're also the most willing, knowing its necessity and the potential for pay-back.

We tend to develop tunnel-vision and blind-spots about our own writing. When it's pointed out, we smack our forehead and say something like, "Yoicks! Why didn't I see that?" Once we're made aware of it, it's as plain as the TransAmerica Pyramid on the San Francisco skyline. We wonder, "How could I have missed it?"

When I have others read my work-in-progress I ask for their input and feedback. I want to know:

• What did I leave out? What did I miss?

• What *should* I have left out?

• Are there inconsistencies where there shouldn't be?

• Is it clearly written and understandable? *(I* know what

I am trying to say, but have I written it so that *you* know what I am trying to say?)

I'm like the 18-wheeler drivers on the highway with their signs asking, "How am I driving?" I'm asking, "How am I writing? How can I write it better?" And I **want** them to tell me.

I don't always follow my editors' suggestions, though. And neither will you. Sometimes they just don't **get** it; they're on a different wavelength or even a different planet from me.

However, while I may ultimately reject their advice, I absolutely appreciate it. I listen and seriously consider each of their suggestions. And if I decide not to use it, at least I've thought it through very carefully and made the decision based on what I believe will work best.

RITE OF PASSAGE

Oliver Green, Colorado Springs, CO

I had by now become thoroughly indoctrinated in Navy tradition and wanted to do everything that would make me "Navy." If a tattoo were a part of the process, so be it.

. . . I had three buddies, all the same age. We were inseparable . . . . We discussed the business of tattoos. One main concern was whether the tattoo would be visible on our skin. All of us were black, but different shades of black.

Big Dave had red hair and a very light complexion. Bob was of mixed blood: half white and half black. Joe was a huge man; he stood 6'5" and was muscular and mean-looking. . . . He was truly the blackest man I had ever seen. Then there was Oliver, who had instigated the tattoo idea.

One evening the four of us headed into town. Norfolk, Virginia. The decision had been made. . . . After a few beers to strengthen our resolve, we decided we'd all get the same tattoo. One more beer and the big four ("All for one and one for all, Navy-tried-and-true") swaggered off to the tattoo parlor.

It was a dingy little place. The owner did not impress us as a reputable character. Nevertheless, we made the selection and the artist began on Big Dave. We flinched, but this was our test. . . . To our surprise, the outline on Big Dave's forearm was beautiful. The artist completed the tattoo by filling in the outline with the red and green and orange colors. I was next. My tattoo application went as easy as Dave's, and Bob followed with no problem. . . . The artist was really skilled in his craft. The four of us cheered.

Then it was Joe's turn. We all wondered if the tattoo would be visible on his black skin. Joe wanted so much to be one of the "big four." The artist looked at Joe's black forearm with a wry expression. He knew the results would not be to his satisfaction, but he proceeded. As he began the outline with the needle, the blue ink was barely visible under the dark skin. The artist shook his head, adding different colors: orange, green and red. Joe was elated with what he thought he was going to have. Finally, the work was completed . . .

. . . To say the least, we were proud of ourselves. We were Navy-tried-and-true. Traditional sailors. We strutted around with our shirtsleeves rolled up to our elbows, displaying our prize possession. Joe did have difficulty showing off his prize. He was most proud. He could be overheard at times, talking to other sailors, pointing to his forearm, asking, "Can't you see it, you damn fool?!" He intimidated people into seeing what was barely visible. They would walk away shaking their heads and mumbling to themselves. They saw something because Joe said it was there. It was hilarious!

. . . Time passes and nothing stays the same. The beautiful colors on the tattoo have faded and gone, as happens to most beauty. Nothing remains now but a blurred outline, a constant reminder of the days growing up on the naval base at St. Juliens Creek, Virginia.

*Published in **55-plus!**, San Francisco, CA, 1996*

GROUP DYNAMICS

Since every writer needs feedback, I recommend joining or forming a class or a writers group which meets regularly. Even a small group of 2 or 3 can be very helpful. In the group you can ask for honest and thoughtful constructive feedback.

In my classes and writing groups I do not allow destructive or 'brutally honest' criticism; that is, criticism for the sake of criticism. I advise writing classes and groups to have some ground rules or agreements in place from the outset. For example, when critiquing one another's writing, I suggest that you make it a point to accentuate the positive; to encourage and support one another.

Please be sensitive to the tender feelings of the writer, whether novice or professional. We are all sensitive and vulnerable regarding our creative efforts.

Remember, in critiquing, as in the rest of life, it's not *what* you say but *how* you say it. Try to find a gentle way to get your point across.

There's a story about Louisa May Alcott, author of *Little Women, Little Men, Jo's Boys, et al)*. Both she and a college friend yearned to be writers and enrolled in writing classes. Alcott's class was supportive, encouraging and positive. Her friend's was not. In his class, blunt criticism was the rule. We all know that Alcott went on to become a very successful author. Her friend did not. He gave up and went into some other profession, feeling like a failed writer before he'd even begun.

Having said that, if your writing group is to be useful to you, it's important that you be open to your fellow writers' constructive suggestions.

My suggested list of ***Do's & Don't's***:

<u>Do</u>:

- ask your fellow-writers to tell you what they like about your story as well as what doesn't work for them, and why.
- ask them to tell you when what you've written is unclear.
- ask them to tell you when you are repetitive/redundant.
- ask them to tell you when you should shorten or expand your story or a part of it.
- tell them if you wish them to correct your grammar and spelling, or not.
- listen to what they have to say; they're trying to help.
- sincerely thank everyone for evaluating your work.
- realize that the final decision is yours. Their suggestions are just that -- suggestions. It is your story and the final version is up to you.

<u>Do not</u>:

• fall in love with your own words. Be willing to consider changing or eliminating some.

• let your ego get in the way of having the best finished product possible.

• get defensive. It's counterproductive.

It's important that you let your group members know what you want from them. If you find that your needs are not being met in your group, exit gracefully and find or start a new one.

Benefits of a Writers Group -- a Win-Win

The benefits of attending a writers group are many. Among the most important is that by attending a regular meeting of writers committed to producing a written work, you are motivated to write something for every meeting. Since the expectation is that everyone will bring something they've written to every meeting, you'll put a little pressure on yourself to write and actually get some work done. The expectation is not that members will bring a perfect piece of writing to the meeting. Bring whatever you're working on in whatever state it's in. That's what the group is for.

I must emphasize, however, the importance of attending regularly, whether you've managed to write something or not. I fully realize, as your fellow writers will, that there are times when life gets in the way and it's impossible to set aside the required amount of time or to get your mind functioning creatively. Go to the meeting anyway, if at all possible. Your fellow writers need your input on their work, and you need the stimulation and inspiration they provide.

A vital function of membership in a writers group is simply that you provide an audience for one anothers' writings and life experiences, thereby validating one anothers' lives.

It's a win-win situation. You're getting your stories written and feeling good about yourself and your life! You can't lose!

Furthermore, consider the fact that writing is a solitary affair. It's lovely to get together with a group of folks who understand and can empathize and laugh with you over the challenges and situations you encounter as an autobiographical writer.

In addition, many a lasting, meaningful friendship has been forged over a weekly 'cuppa' and the discussion of manuscripts in progress.

Writers' Class/Group Methods

Writers' groups and classes operate differently.

In some, each writer makes a copy of that week's work for every other member. The members take all the writings home and evaluate them, with notes in the margins or a longer note on the back. The following week the author reads that work aloud. Verbal response is then requested and accepted. Or the author takes home all the evaluations prepared by fellow class members and reads them in solitude.

Other groups simply have each member read his or her work aloud, and the others respond on the spot.

Both methods are productive and useful. The first

offers more specific assistance while the latter is more for support and encouragement. Some groups very effectively combine the two.

Class or Group Size

Most people, especially beginning writers, feel less intimidated in smaller groups. In addition, since time is limited, if the group is small everyone gets a chance to read his or her work and get feedback, which is why you're there, after all.

I find that it works best to limit the size of classes to 10 - 15. Larger classes of any size can work if they break into smaller groups when it's time for individual support and evaluation.

For informal over-the-kitchen-table writers' groups, 3 - 5 seems the most productive.

An invention; fads, styles

ODE TO HAIRSPRAY

Effie Marie Larsen, Burlingame, CA

In bygone times before hairspray
    every day was a bad hair day.
Every style was so damn trying
    it would have me cursin' 'n' crying.
With many a clippie and bobby pin,
    each blessed day would end and begin.
Rinses of vinegar, milk, even beer,
    they did no good, not even near.
Big silken scarves protecting our curls
    from the damp fog and windy swirls,
covered the heads of all of us girls,
    enroute to school, jobs and social whirls.
Late in the 50's there came a strange style
    of hair up in rollers 'most all of the while
for shopping, appointments and PTA meetings,
    so later on, Hubby'd bestow loving greetings.
This limp, wispy hair -- my bane of existence!
    How I'd pray with impassioned insistence
for deliverance, for divine intervention,
    when Hallelujah! there was an invention.
It came in a spray can for swift application
    and changed women's lives all over the nation.
We comb, spray and run, out the door in a jiffy,
    each hair in place, curled, fluffed and spiffy.
In my book, hairspray is as much of a boon
    as penicillin, PCs and trips to the moon.
Now 'nary a day goes by I don't bless
    the inventor of hairspray -- a woman, I'd guess.

READING ALOUD ALLOWED

Not only is reading aloud allowed, it's downright essential. Whether or not you're in a writers group, make it a practice to read what you've written out loud. It's an excellent method of self-editing. By vocalizing it, using two senses rather than one, you'll have a greater chance of catching errors, and you'll be better able to hear how it works in general.

But it's best to read your work to someone else, if possible. When you have an audience your critical senses become more acute. And you may elicit editing suggestions from your listener, as well.

Although you may think you are imposing upon your friends, chances are excellent that they will be honored and delighted to listen to you read about your life's adventures. They'll be amazed to learn things about you they never imagined!

WILL IT SURVIVE TECHNOLOGY?

Why not just tape record your life stories? Telling them into a tape recorder or camcorder is wonderful, and I heartily recommend it, but **ONLY in addition to getting it in writing.**

Tapes and CDs or DVDs can wear out, fade, break or otherwise self-destruct. Also, in this era of speed-of-light technological advancement, I can't help wondering how long the instruments on which we play the current types of audio cassettes, videos, CD's and DVD's will be available. Your descendants may end up with a bunch of recorded memoirs that are useless because they can no longer listen to or view them.

Think, for example, of vinyl phonograph records, 8-track tapes or the Beta videos. It is now virtually impossible to find an instrument on which to play them or, if you are lucky enough to get one, to find someone who can repair and maintain it. If your memoirs were recorded on them, think of the challenge it would present to someone a couple of generations from now, just to try to listen to or watch them. The same sort of difficulty is probable with our current recording methods.

Imagine that you are placing your taped or filmed memoirs in a time capsule, to be opened 50 or 100 years from now. Imagine the frustration when someone opens it and realizes that a priceless treasure has been unearthed but there is no way of gaining access to it.

(If you do record your memoirs on audio or video devices, be sure to transfer them onto the latest technology every time it changes (e.g., if your home movies are on videos, get them transferred onto DVDs now. And when the next generation of technology arrives, have them transferred again, from DVD to whatever that is. Better safe than sorry.)

In my opinion, the written word has a far greater chance of surviving the ages and technological advancements. I doubt that books will ever go out of style. So I hope you'll take the time (or get someone else to) to put your memoirs in writing, thereby leaving them in a form that will survive not only the ravages of time but also of technology.

If you're using a computer I'm sure I don't need to tell you to SAVE, SAVE, SAVE, and to back everything up on a diskette at the end of every writing session. Do not assume that because you have it on your computer's hard drive, backed up on a disk, it is safe. Take my word for it, it is not.

*Make printed copies of everything and
keep them in at least 2 different locations.*

Writing Activity:

Write about a turning point in your life; an event or ongoing situation which caused you to change your life's course.

- Write about:
  - Your 'moment of truth':
    - ▲ Give background; describe the series of events that led up to it.
    - ▲ If other people were involved, tell about them and their part in it.
    - ▲ What was 'the last straw'; the point at which you said, "I'm mad as hell and I'm not going to take it anymore," -- or whatever you said.
    - ▲ Your thoughts and feelings: your frustration, anger, depression, hopelessness.
    - ▲ Your 'Aha!' that let you know things could be different.
    - ▲ How it changed your life:
      - ○ Your decision and the actions you took.
      - ○ The results: where/who you are now in your life because of it.
- Paint word-pictures:
  - Bring in the 5 senses.
  - Bring your reader into the scene with you.
- Answer the '6 W's':
  - Who, What, Where, When, Why & How.
- Use 'Spice Up Your Life' techniques (Page 46).
- Have fun!

TIME'S A-WASTIN'

Tick tock . . . . .

        Tick tock . . . . .

                Tick tock . . . . . .

Time's a-wastin'.

So just do it. Just get started . . . and just get it done.

You'll be glad you did. And so will those who love you -- both those who know you personally in the here and now, and those who will come to know and love you through your memoir . . . . . somewhere in time.

        Tick tock . . . . .

                Tick tock . . . . .

                        Tick tock . . .

Once upon a time . . ..

Appendix

90 WAYS TO SAY "SAID"

There is nothing wrong with simply writing, ". . . he said." But there are other ways of saying it, so if you'd like to add variety in writing dialogue, here are a few:

uttered	vocalized	announced
spoke	mouthed	phrased
answered	responded	replied
rejoined	retorted	remarked
came out with	communicated	conveyed
stated	declared	told
imparted	presented	mentioned
added	informed	revealed
let out	divulged	disclosed
made known	cried	breathed
whispered	gasped	repeated
recited	orated	delivered
groaned	estimated	predicted
predicated	speculated	hypothesized
conjectured	explained	assumed
judged	imagined	promised
implied	reported	alleged
avered	avowed	attested
testified	certified	vouched
bore witness	requested	lied
warranted	professed	claimed
purported	pretended	imputed
insinuated	cited	assigned
advanced	offered	proposed
pleaded	echoed	acknowledged
shouted	hollered	screamed
commanded	ordered	dictated
surmised	related	advised
emphasized	emoted	pointed out
commented	reasoned	admitted

EMOTIION-WORDS

A therapist for many years, I asked my clients to talk about their feelings. In many cases, they didn't have the vocabulary or needed help identifying their emotions. The following is a list of *'feeling words'* I compiled to help them. Maybe it will help you, too, in writing about your own and others' feelings, e.g: "I felt ....", or "He seemed ...."

happy	pleased	joyful
delighted	glad	contented
cheerful	light-hearted	optimistic
jovial	exultant	exuberant
jolly	elated	thrilled
gleeful	euphoric	on cloud nine
proud	satisfied	gratified
lucky	fortunate	grateful
prosperous	appreciative	blessed
powerful	successful	strong
forceful	invincible	robust
rugged	tough	virile
dynamic	vigorous	lusty
significant	important	energetic
trusting	believing	confident
loyal	honest	reliable
honorable	aboveboard	tried & true
ethical	moral	virtuous
positive	naive	gullible
affectionate	loving	adoring
passionate	infatuated	in love
longing	pining	aroused
rapturous	romantic	attractive
formidable	courageous	brave
bold	fearless	determined
lionhearted	spunky	tireless

purposeful	practical	decisive
generous	giving	altruistic
benevolent	unselfish	humane
encouraged	heartened	uplifted
inspired	motivated	psyched up
enthusiastic	excited	vivacious
bubbling over	fanatical	stunned
surprised	amazed	stupefied
astounded	dazed	dumfounded
powerless	helpless	useless
worthless	futile	dependent
weak	feeble	defenseless
suspicious	doubtful	distrustful
leery	nervous	anxious
uncertain	shy	inhibited
uneasy	fearful	scared
scared stiff	jumpy	squeamish
wary	terrified	frightened
alarmed	startled	intimidated
panicked	horrified	astounded
stunned	disappointed	scandalized
outraged	disgusted	nauseated
repulsed	grossed out	freaked out
intimidated	bullied	browbeaten
upset	stressed	shook up
restless	defiant	rebellious
unruly	wild	incorrigible
hurt	angry	irate
enraged	furious	livid
fuming	distraught	hysterical
feverish	white hot	fit to be tied
rabid	mad	peeved
annoyed	irrational	spiteful
unreasonable	childish	temperamental

silly	refreshed	fit as a fiddle
irritated	galled	hot-headed
cranky	ill-tempered	frantic
quarrelsome	cantankerous	irascible
hostile	belligerent	antagonistic
contrary	aggressive	unfriendly
unkind	unsociable	inhibited
mean	small-minded	ungenerous
nasty	sinister	diabolical
repugnance	rancorous	bitter
vain	self-important	snooty
full of himself	self-absorbed	snobbish
aloof	indifferent	pompous
disloyal	untrue	deceitful
hateful	vicious	spiteful
stingy	tight-fisted	jealous
resentful	envious	yearning
vigilant	mindful	cautious
insecure	threatened	vulnerable
inept	inappropriate	foolish
awkward	oafish	absurd
incompetent	inadequate	immoral
corrupt	depraved	villainous
perverted	lecherous	horny
salacious	hot	rakish
crazy	insane	bonkers
schizoid	berserk	asinine
sad	weepy	depressed
despondent	gloomy	crushed
heartbroken	down in the dumps	low
confused	bewildered	mystified
perplexed	puzzled	baffled
ashamed	embarrassed	humiliated
sorry	bummed	miserable
wretched	guilty	sympathetic

Writing Activity:
Write a story in which your career or a job is featured.

◆ Write about:
- your brilliant career.
- the best/worst job you ever had.
- the weirdest job you ever had.
- the most rewarding job you ever had.
- the most punishing job you ever had.
- your first job.

◆ Tell how you got into that line of work or how you got that particular job.

◆ Show anecdotally why it was the best (worst, weirdest, etc.) job you ever had.

◆ Have fun!

Writing Activity:
Write your love story.

◆ Write about:
- how you met the love of your life.
- what made him/her stand out from the crowd.
- the courtship.
- endearing habits, traits, mannerisms.
- less-than-endearing habits, traits, mannerisms
- difficulties or challenges you experienced.
- how your families & friends felt about your relationship.
- the outcome:
  - ▲ short term & long term

◆ Have fun!

Writing Activity:

◆ Write a story about the best/worst advice you ever got:
- the circumstances in which it was given.
- the person who gave it to you.
  - ▲ your relationship.
  - ▲ how/why he/she happened to give it to you.
- your decision to heed the advice, or not.
- your subsequent actions.
- difficulties or challenges you experienced.
- other people who were affected by it.
  - ▲ how they felt and reacted
- the outcome (how your life was affected by it):
  - ▲ short term & longterm
◆ Have fun!

Writing Activity:

Write a story about synchronicity and/or serendipity (a coincidence bordering on the miraculous, and/or an unexpected happy occurrence).

(Coincidence is God's way of performing a miracle.)

We all have had amazing, inexplicable, paradoxical happenings in our lives that leave us scratching our heads and wondering about the nature of the universe.

Write about one of those happenings. Be sure to include all the mystery, the wonder, the awe of it.

Use the appropriate techniques from this text to make your story engaging.

Have fun!

Writing Activity:

◆ Write about how your life has turned out different than you'd expected. This could be from the perspective of yourself at any stage of life:
- the present: an overview of your whole life.
- a time of transition:
  ▲ starting school (or a new school)
  ▲ your job or career
  ▲ marriage
  ▲ family life (children, grandchildren)
  ▲ retirement
  ▲ 'living your dream', *et cetera*
◆ Tell what you expected and what you got.
◆ Write your emotions: bewilderment, confusion, anger, disappointment, delight, surprise, fulfillment.

Writing Activity:

Write about your spiritual journey. (This could be an essay or a story -- or a combination.)

◆ Write about your beliefs:
- Where you started out (your parents' religion or belief-system?)
- What happened to change or reinforce that.
  ▲ your 'aha!'s.
  ▲ people who influenced your beliefs, one way or the other.
  ▲ religious affiliations (if any).
◆ Be as anecdotal as you can.
◆ Tell what you believe about the nature of God and/or the universe, and why. Be specific.

◆ Have fun!

ABOUT THE AUTHOR

Carol Petersen Purroy has taught her memoir-writing class since 1991, inspiring and helping hundreds of people of all ages to write their life stories. She now teaches this class and others at Truckee Meadows Community College in northern Nevada. She is a freelance writer and writes a column for senior magazines.

Her careers have included Publisher/Editor, Writer, Teacher, Reading Specialist, Psychotherapist/Clinical Hypnotherapist and Disaster Relief Worker.

She was born and grew up in California's San Joaquin Valley, married at 18, and had three sons. At 34, she re-entered the academic world, earning a B.A. in Anthropology, Teaching Credentials, and an M.A. in Psychology.

She lives in Reno, NV., is the grandmother of one, mentor, "Mom" and "Grandma Carol" to many others.